There's Wonder Around the Bend

Published by WonderBing Books
275 Cumberland Parkway #262
Mechanicsburg, PA. 17055

ISBN: 979-8-9903614-0-9 (hardcover)
ISBN: 979-8-9903614-1-6 (paperback)
ISBN: 979-8-9903614-2-3 (eBook)

Cover and interior design by Melissa Williams Design

Praise for
There's Wonder Around the Bend

There's Wonder Around the Bend gently guides the reader to discover or perhaps rediscover those things that bring wonder into our lives through travel. Using her easy and descriptive writing style, Beth takes the reader on a journey exploring the *why go* as well as the *how do I do this*? As an experienced road tripper, I learned new things that will make my trips better. Prepare yourself for exciting new adventures—it's easier than you think.

—Marlene Pankey Hale, author of
Sara's Story, the Amazing Grace of God

Beth is a storyteller at heart, which gives her book an added richness. You'll learn much about solo road tripping while being invited to join her on the path to wonder.

—Elaine Bonds, MABS Dallas theological seminary

Occasionally, you read a book you didn't know you needed to read until after you have finished. This is that book! Beth's book challenged me to look beyond my every day and consider how exciting and rewarding it could be to spend a little time seeking wonder! I am going to plan a trip all on my own; I can't wait to find what's around the bend for me!

—Karen Dougherty

So much more than a guidebook, Beth Binger's *There's Wonder Around the Bend* is a very personal invitation to find deep sigh contentment on the open road. Don't worry; there are plenty of practical trips to equip you to roam confidently. But the joy in the journey—the God-gifted wonder around the bend—is always the steady heartbeat of a book that reads like a life-giving conversation between old friends.

—Kathy Wingert

There's *Wonder* Around the Bend

An Inspiring Guide to Solo Road Tripping

Beth Binger

To my parents,

Thank you for a childhood chock-full of the
wonder of unlimited library books and the
freedom of outdoor adventure.

Please visit

www.wonderbingtravel.com/book-resources

to download the additional resources
mentioned throughout the book.

Contents

Part One

The Road to Wonder

Foreword

The golden light of the West Virginia summer sunset bounced up and down in my rearview mirror, mountains ahead all lavender pinks as I sped into the coming darkness. Lexi, my then 10-month-old golden retriever, sprawled peacefully in the back seat. After 3 weeks, 13 states, and 5,000 slow and glorious miles, I was exhausted and ready to fall into my own bed. That afternoon, I broke my self-imposed no-highway rule and hopped on Routes 64 and 81 in an effort to arrive before midnight.

I was at peace and my mind at rest. Inky blackness settled around me and I sifted through the events of the last weeks and even years. The mostly uninhabited and endless dark highway provided space and permission to turn my thoughts inward for the first time in a while. There are many reasons why I avoid highways on a road trip. Life doesn't really happen on an interstate, and there's rarely anything of import to observe. John Steinbeck reflected as he set out on his extended American road trip, "I stayed as much as possible on secondary roads where there was much to hear and see and smell, and avoided the great wide traffic slashes which promote the self by fostering daydreams."[1] Yes and amen, my point exactly. Except there I was on this night, musing away into daydreaming.

At some point "inspiration," if you can call it that, struck, or at least began to prick at the edges of my imagination. I was listening back to the voices of many women who inquired about my adventures. Some belonged to those met in far-flung places across the country, while others weighed in on my blog or social media. Perhaps the most vocal group was also the most faithful contingent—family and friends. Their questions began pinging around the silence of my SUV.

"Aren't you afraid to travel alone?" "How do you plan for something like that—isn't it overwhelming?" The wistful, "I wish I could do that" or more urgent, "I desperately need to do something like that, but I don't know how." The doubt-filled, "I'm not brave enough, strong enough, confident enough." And the slightly apprehensive, yet hope-filled, "I've never been away on my own." Wherever I turned, these sentiments surfaced. The most frequent comment was always some rendition of, "Save me a seat next time—I'd love to come with you!"

In those voices, I could hear passion. Sometimes longing. Even sadness. Perhaps, occasionally, jealousy, only because they didn't think these experiences could ever be theirs. The recognition of something they wanted, needed, but hadn't given a name before. Some seemed to need only structure for their sense of adventure to blossom into action. Others sought permission.

Slashing across that barren highway, it occurred to me that I could help these women fulfill their desire to "just go." I could offer practical guidance as well as encouragement for women who feel too overwhelmed by the process to strike out on their own but know they crave just a bit of personal adventure. After all, it was on the road that I found freedom and reclaimed joy. Wouldn't it be an honor and a joy to equip others who want the same?

And so, the idea of *There's Wonder Around the Bend* was born, roughly at the juncture of Routes 64 and 81 in central Virginia, not far from the mountain town of Lexington. This place and name are significant as the town is also the namesake of Lexi the Golden, my faithful traveling companion. Officially named Lexington Hope, Lexi has logged almost as many miles as I have in the past several years.

For all the importance the name Lexington holds for me, it seemed perfect that the location would mark another birth of sorts. In roughly the same place where I was gifted with a golden girl who proved to be the catalyst to fix a broken heart, God revealed a way forward with a new dream and opportunity to serve others.

Not surprisingly, within weeks (if not hours) of arriving home, regular life began to overshadow my dream of writing this book. My clear mind blurred with the infusion of family, house, job, errands, and the necessary details of life. Weeks of travel, freedom, and wonder drifted into the background.

Though I never let go of the idea for the book, it lay dormant for much of the year to follow. And I doubted. Does the world really need a women's guide to road-tripping? Hasn't someone already done this? I tested, researched, thought, and prayed some more. Ultimately, I determined this little book could fill a void and provide the tools and perhaps the motivation for women to strike out confidently on their own.

But the work, as I turned to it, now felt stale. Something was missing. Reflecting on my travels, I asked myself what that longing I had first responded to, and that others had responded to, was all about. There I found the missing piece. I had been thinking about all the "hows" and "wheres" of travel. How could I possibly have ignored the "why"?

Guidebooks by their very nature are pretty cut-and-dried, and, initially, that is how I viewed this project. Pack this, go here, buy those, find that, and mix in a bit of "rah, rah, you can do it, yes you can!" My book would be practical, with ideas and links and lists, and remove from the process much of the intimidation of planning for those who needed guidance.

But what about joy? and freedom? and wonder? Lessons far more compelling and life-altering. This is the heart of why road trips fulfill me in so many ways, and I believe these feelings are what other women had responded to. I had rushed ahead in my mind with thoughts of how to help, but in doing so, I had set aside what was at the very heart of it all for more pragmatic pursuits. What if women followed all the how-to instructions but were left feeling empty and, even worse, paralyzed from planning? No. That wouldn't do at all. The prize is in the pursuit of wonder, and that must not be lost.

My compass reset, I realized that I needed to help people dig deeper. Surely, I could help equip women to plan and execute a road trip. And if that's where it ended, those necessities would prove useful to those who want checklists and directions. But a road trip for me is never about getting from point A to point B, well-fortified with snacks and a great GPS. Never. It isn't even the stops along the way, though that's certainly part of it.

In the chapters to come, you will find everything you need to figure out where you're going, what to take, how to budget and employ safety measures, how to navigate your meals and lodging, and on and on. It's all here, and it is all vitally integral to preparing to go out confidently on your own, maybe for the first time. This was, after all, the entire initial brainstorm for this book. And it is my delight to share everything I have learned these past years as a solo road-tripper and a long-time traveler in general.

*But the how-tos only provide
the tools to experience the real joy—
the pursuit of wonder.*

So, this is where the road divides—where we part ways from the traditional guidebook. I am living proof, tens of thousands of miles and almost 50 states worth of proof, that, at the heart of the solo American road trip, you will not find mere maps and lists and half-eaten granola bars. No. You'll discover the glory in God's creation, joy, wonder, freedom, and, whether you're searching or not, you'll undoubtedly find a little more of YOU.

Chapter 1

Priming for Wonder

The early morning dawns fresh and inviting, warm light creeping over the hill across the road and beckoning me to rise and get on with it. No need for further encouragement. I'm up—my mind already far ahead of my unfolding and increasingly creaky body. Today is The Day. The car waits, packed like a stuffed sausage, and I hear Lexi the Golden shake herself awake in the growing light, knowing instinctively that *something* is about to happen. She's anxious to confirm she will not be left behind.

Every Day One of a road trip starts like this: senses heightened, excitement palpable, the promise of impending adventure, and an undeniable desire to chase and embrace both freedom and wonder. My heart pounds a little just typing the words. Can you feel it too?

Embarking on a road trip is akin to reading the most gripping mystery novel. Every bend in the road is a page with a new secret to uncover, character to be introduced, setting to be soaked in. There are hints as to how it may play out, but complete immersion is the only means to unveil the layers of the not yet known. That's where the joy lives—in the daily unfurling of the journey itself.

I begin every day of a road trip with the same eagerness—seeing each as a new chapter in the mystery of the adventure. The analogy fails in regard to pace, however. Unlike when reading, I do not anxiously speed ahead to the next bit of discovery, but rather, leisurely relish every sight and sound. Slow and easy. This gentler pace allows every day of every road trip I've ever taken to etch itself in my memory—where each day begins, where it ends, engraving countless details from sunup to sundown. The impressions are deep and permanent, each passing mile providing increasing clarity of spirit and mind.

Being on the road by myself creates daily opportunity not only to slow down, but to be purposeful. And in that wide open space, I am able to embrace the two greatest gifts of the solo adventure—unending possibilities to find freedom and to experience wonder.

I find freedom on the road. The freedom of mind—freedom *from* regular life, freedom *to* see the details of the world outside my moving window or on a slow walk where my feet tread the unknown. The cobwebs of normal busyness dissolve in the wind, left behind in the dust, usurped by a freeing clarity. I look ahead, above, beside, but not back. I look down, not at my own little self, but at the road beneath my feet. The world widens and grows, and I become smaller within it. And in that vastness, I feel it—Freedom.

And, ultimately, wonder. It emerges in varied forms. Wonder may take the unexpected and powerful form of a grizzly running across a Montana road, the purples of a sunset blazing fire across the waters of Lake Superior, or the simple sweetness of a wizened shopkeeper sharing morning greetings with customers and friends as he likely has been doing decade upon decade. Like freedom, wonder is found in the looking-out part, eyes wide open, heart anticipating each new discovery. I find wonder around every turn.

In my road-tripping world, freedom and wonder preside over each day, each moment. Traveling taps into my senses and awareness like no other experience and inscribes permanent souvenirs into my soul. It's where I learn the most about myself while not paying myself any attention at all.

As a Christian, I experience each of these moments with gratitude for God's perfect creation. That I have the privilege to witness so much of it, firsthand, brings me to my knees and leaves me breathless. And in my smallness, I marvel also in knowing that our God declared all of His creation to be good, yet, somehow, His love for us, His people, is such that He created us in His own image to be *very* good. Grace upon grace. Mystery. Inexplicable and humbling.

And, also, intoxicating. God's unending love and care for my completely undeserving self lead me to know that it matters how I spend my time, what I think, and how I engage with His creation. Travel emerges as a most natural response, an act of worship, and I have embraced the realization of this dormant passion to revel in what He has made. It becomes a quiet and powerful way to seek Him, to be in communion with Him, to be thankful and grateful for all He has done. As God reveals Himself to me around every bend, I learn more and more about who I am called to be. Resting in the surety that I humbly bear His image, I begin to discern and embrace the gifts He has given me.

Freedom and Wonder

*A road trip is a freedom journey that
moves you from wandering to wonder.*

The words "road trip" likely conjure visions of windows down, hair flying, destination unknown without a care in the world. We love the romantic notion of wandering without a plan—the appeal strong, as it stands in stark contrast to our everyday structured and plotted days. And it is worth dreaming about. We want that feeling. Reckless abandon maybe? Carefree with no schedule? Perhaps a bit of escape? Yes, yes, and yes.

But I believe there's more. I know there is. Carefree escapism and reckless abandon can be an incredibly fun piece of it, but shortly after returning home, you'll likely feel lost and empty and back in the mud puddle you left in the first place. In fact, my own journey began as an instinctive desire to wander, but ultimately propelled me toward wonder.

Not long before my initial road-tripping adventure, much of the decades-long familiarity of my world disappeared. My children were mostly grown, and my husband of a quarter century moved on to another life and another wife. Everything seemed to shift from the familiar, if not always comfortable, to a landscape akilter, propelling me into unexpected and unknown territory. Those first uncertain months on my own, filled with rickety, shaky moments, came on the heels of several years in which our family careened back and forth between periods of normalcy and deep, dark cycles where home-preservation meant gingerly navigating the crazy-making. An existence that was one moment comfortable and pleasant could turn on a dime into the frightening and wildly unpredictable. And then, in an extraordinary paradox of slow motion and a shocking flash, I was starting anew.

The disruption bore the markings of an earthquake, everything that had seemed solid suddenly jiggling about and coming loose. My instinct was to hold onto the most precious—my children—and attempt to keep them free from harm. All the while I was falling, tumbling forward through the upheaval of a lost husband, home, identity. As is the way with natural disasters, the dust eventually settled. At least enough to take stock. There was damage, and a need to rebuild.

I doubt I could have eloquently expressed why a road trip was such a clear and natural next step in my life. It wasn't an attempt to find a solution or resolution to a problem I couldn't fix, and I certainly had no clue that it would serve as the catalyst for me to regain my footing and put the pieces of my world back into perspective. I just did it. Somehow it emerged as the most logical, comforting, and right next thing to do, and not because I had a history of solo road-tripping. Nope. I had spent most of the previous 25 years being a fully present mom and wife. Vacation typically meant heading for the beach, where I happily continued to be mom and wife but with sand in every crevice of person, car, and rental home. Occasionally, it meant flying off with my husband on a work-sponsored trip to a beautiful destination, miles traversed above clouds. Yet, in my newly disordered world, the simple ribbon of road beckoned. And I just went.

What I know now: that first solo road trip filled a deep need. A need to be other-focused. To look out and not in. A need to let the creation of my great and glorious God wash over me, as He protected and provided for me each mile marker and step of the way. Despite my uncertain future, extended time on that journey turned my focus away from myself. I didn't need more of me, but less. I needed more of Him.

I began each day on the road, praying the words Jeremy Camp wrote in his song, "Keep Me in the Moment."

> Oh Lord, keep me in the moment
> Help me live with my eyes wide open
> 'Cause I don't want to miss what you have for me
> Oh Lord, show me what matters
> Throw away what I'm chasing after
> 'Cause I don't want to miss what you have for me.

And my favorite line:

> All I got is one shot, one try
> One go around in this beautiful life
> Nothing is wasted when everything's placed in your hands.[1]

I slowed way, way down, took time, opened my eyes and my ears. I shut my mouth, turned off the noise in my head (and on my phone), and began to look around. By looking *out*, I slowly discovered all those lost parts of myself. Little by little, mile after mile. It was a journey of reclamation, of shedding what had bound and diminished me, and of pursuing wonder. I took the back roads. I noticed every little thing. Even the smallest details of that first trip are burned in my memory forever. The experience was healing, intoxicating, and transformative.

The pursuit of wonder has altered my perspective. Not

just in those soul-shifting moments when something takes my breath away, but as those moments take their place in the larger context, as the sum of an entire experience that has the power to affect how I think, how I experience the glory of God and my role in response to Him and His love. As God's healing worked in me, the wall I had built around my spirit as a means of holding myself and my world together began to crack and light got through. I began to see with anticipation, looking for what God had to show me next. Initially I didn't know what, if anything, I was searching for, but as the miles piled up behind me and I eagerly anticipated all that was in front of me, I began to shed layers of dust, daily grime, heavy burden, fear, and loss. I became lighter, awake, aware, and free. I could taste joy and touch wonder, both as real as the afternoon sun.

Your story is uniquely your own. My own narrative may or may not resonate with you, but hopefully it inspires you to see a way forward—a path to dream. Your life may not be undergoing a seismic shift—you may be in search of a fresh perspective or you ache to recover a sense of purpose or to uncover the art within your soul or to see anew. All of these are reasons to pursue wonder. To step out, watching. Listening. Seeking.

The goal of this book is to help you
uncover your own freedom and wonder,
and to employ the pragmatic pieces of
organization, research, and planning to
confidently set out on your own.
To keep your eyes wide open to
what God has for you.

And as you head out, knowing that you've prepared and that you've got this, the most wonderful thing will happen. You will begin to breathe more deeply, see more clearly. You'll discover that you are surrounded by wonder. You'll regain the lost art, not just of noticing what's around you, but likely *discovering* that the formerly mundane or unremarkable bears the mark of the sublime.

In this, there is joy. And peace. (And dare I add, relief?) I have experienced firsthand the next natural outpouring of those moments: overwhelming gratitude and thanksgiving for the intricate simplicities of the world around me. I consistently learn that purposeful and slow doesn't have to be a lost way of living. The opportunity to engage in our world this way is a standing invitation from our Creator. After all, it's all right there in front of us, waiting to be noticed. In my world, that deserves declarations, both whispered and shouted, of "Thank You, Jesus!" At the very least, I'll put my money on you being reduced to stillness and, it may surprise you, tears at least once.

So, when you've embraced the inspiring bit and followed through on the practicalities shared in the coming pages, you'll know how to get in the car and go without worrying you'll make a mess of it. You'll be confident, maybe a little nervous, but excited. You'll have all kinds of tips and tools to make it work well. You'll understand that good planning (to the extent that it makes you happy and not stressed out) is a big piece of finding contentment on the road.

You'll be primed and ready for wonder.

Chapter 2

Wonder

I wonder. Two little words that not only spark joy in my soul but call me to action. Wonder fuels me. I even love the sound of the word as it tumbles out of my mouth, creating its own energy. Wonder is both noun and verb, past and future. It simultaneously recalls the simplicity of childhood and well-worn wistful longings in this too-busy life. I ache for it in the present.

When I went in search of a working definition of "wonder," my favorite by far came from Oxford Languages.

> **Wonder:** (noun) a feeling of surprise mingled with admiration, caused by something beautiful, unexpected, unfamiliar, or inexplicable.

Gosh, yes, and please may I have some more! It's Christmas when you're five, all wide eyes and expectation, the promise of something unimaginably exciting if you can just be patient for one more day. It's walking down the aisle on your wedding day, overflowing joy-filled hearts on either side and your beloved beaming with bright misty eyes. The first steps of your child, the golden days' end light on fresh snow, piles of puppies tumbling in the leaves. It's all wonder. Beautiful, unexpected, unfamiliar, inexplicable. Let's keep that feeling close as we forge ahead together in the pursuit of reconnecting with the marvelous gift of wonder.

The Simple Past

Every one of us is motivated in large part by collected pieces of our younger selves. Our dreams, desires, and disappointments of today likely stem from experiences of our youth. We grow up and carve out lives that tend either to resemble our upbringing or totally deviate from it. Marriage, careers, worldly success, children of your own, and perhaps tragedy, loss, and big regret may fit into your puzzle somewhere. The simplicity and joy of childhood are apt to slip far into the background most days as you navigate the intricacies of the here and now.

Not everyone carries sweet memories of youth, nor does coming of age require heartbreak and burden. Many of us, however, likely consider our childhoods as simpler times in our lives. Mine certainly was. It was filled with the wonder that was part of the fabric of the uncomplicated every day. Maybe your connection to wonder remains from your college days or those early years on your own, when the world was there for the taking. While the history of our experiences differs, I dare say that somewhere along the line you have experienced a season of wonder—a time when your world seemed simple, your mind fresh and free, eyes open to embrace the day with little thought or concern for the complications that may now weigh you down.

As the idea of this book has slowly settled in my mind, I have thought quite a bit about my own route, if you will, from childhood through the ups and downs of adulthood. I've realized that the impetus behind this writing is inherently connected to reclaiming the feeling of wonder found in the simplicity of childhood, before I knew too much, before life grew muddy and complex. Part of my journey in uncovering wonder in my current life has involved sitting with my own memories a bit. I'll share with you how God prepared me over time to be ready to revel in these moments. Perhaps it will inspire you as you seek the next brave steps in your own unique world.

A Journey of Faith

I wish to be transparent with you—to share with you openly and honestly—both the beauty and the tough stuff. I am a Christian. There are plenty of other words to describe me, and you'll undoubtedly learn a decent bit about me through these pages, but this one fact colors my world. It shapes how I think and transcends pretty much everything. I cannot separate myself from my saving faith in Jesus any more than I can change who my parents are or that I grew up in Central Pennsylvania.

As I pursue wonder, I cannot separate that wonder from the God who created all of it. Consider this: when you encounter something that takes your breath away and brings you to your knees, tears welling in your eyes, it is God-created. And as He created, He looked and saw and declared that it was "good" and for our benefit. God's handiwork serves as a way for us to see and experience Him in the world. Creation is a reflection of Him, and pursuing wonder in His creation is simply a form of worship.

But God didn't stop creating after day five. We too are His creation—his pièce de résistance! We are the miracle-of-the-sixth-day, created-and-declared-*very*-good, and made-in-His-divine-image creation. As magnificent and show-stopping as may be the sky and mountains and oceans and animals that are so often the subject of our wonder, they remain firmly in the "good" category. But God chose to mark us with distinction, even in the face of His mighty and precious creation thus far. We were created by Him in His likeness—and it is a mark of His love for us that He looked and saw and pronounced this work "very good." How amazing, how humbling, how marvelous is that? Gets me every time.[1]

I recognize that you may not share my perspective, but I believe that you can still uncover a sense of freedom and wonder in your world as you consider and pour through all that is shared in this guide. My gratitude for God's great gifts of creation and of His Son will affect how I share what I've learned. And it is in part because of these great gifts that I believe there is a future for you that includes joy and freedom and a simpler look at life if you want it. This book isn't designed to solve all your problems, but I'm praying it will offer perspective and help you find a way forward.

The Hopeful Future

By now you may want to flip that wonder switch and get on with things, but perhaps you feel unsure that you can move forward in hope. Maybe you're searching, in a rut, just plain burned out—uncertain if there is wonder in your future that will resuscitate your weary body and soul. Please be encouraged by these words of the prophet Jeremiah, spoken centuries ago to God's chosen people: 'For I know the plans I have for you,' declares the Lord, 'plans to prosper you and not to harm you, plans to give you a hope and a future.' —Jeremiah 29:11

Whether these words are fresh and new or life-long companions, I believe they still apply today. Trust that you do have a hope and a future—a hope-full future! Dare to take the next step, and then the next, and see where it leads.

That next step can propel you forward with expectation and hope on a path to reclaim innocence, joy, and wonder in your own life. I believe that we can recover the lost sense of wonder in our lives and embrace an intentional new perspective, recalling what we used to know about ourselves and our world. Remembrance of a time when we could slow down long enough to see beauty in the simple, when life was less cluttered. I'm banking that you remember how that feels, and you want to experience it anew.

For some of us that may require conquering a bit of fear. Perhaps it feels as though thick blankets of fog stifle and prevent you from considering the possibility of finding hope as you move forward. In Sarah Young's timeless devotional, *Jesus Calling,* in which she writes to us from the point of view of Jesus as she knows Him from God's Word, Sarah suggests an alternative perspective on fog. Not as a negative, an irritant, or obstruction (as I tend often to think of it), but as a necessary ingredient in stepping forward in faith, a means to finding our footing in today. She turns the negative on its head and provides readers with a hopeful perspective and peaceful reminder that we need only to see what is in the immediate present, confident because we are in the presence of God, who knows the way through.

As you look again at the path ahead, you notice that a peaceful fog has settled over it, obscuring your view. You can see only a few steps in front of you, so you turn your attention more fully to Me and begin to enjoy My presence. The fog is a protection for you, calling you back into the present moment.

—Sarah Young, *Jesus Calling*[2]

Perhaps this vision of finding peace in your present will help settle your mind, reminding you God knows the way through and will lead you there if you'll let Him. You don't need to know where you're going just yet! And there may be other fears. I get it. All those fears (yours and mine!) are in large part what led me to write this book. We're going to do this together, and I'm here to help every step of the way.

Ultimately, embarking on a journey may just be the catalyst to leaving those fears behind, or at least reining them in. When you're ready to move forward and anticipate your tomorrow, the chapters ahead will guide you through it. The experience of pursuing wonder entails creating an environment where you are ready to proceed with open eyes, truly ready to slow down, to "taste and see that the Lord is good,"[3] and that His creation is wonder-filled.

Much of *There's Wonder Around the Bend* is designed to build a foundation of hope and anticipation as you learn the practical "how-tos" of confidently packing up and heading out on your own. In the end, those tools will lay the groundwork for you to travel freely and experience wonder.

My Wonder Years

As I think back to my path of reclaiming wonder in the world and in my life, it's not that difficult to pin down a few pivotal experiences that absolutely influenced how I arrived in this place. And, yes, I mean physical location, but also a place of peace and joy and anticipation for each day. My life has hardly been distinctive, and it's likely these moments from my life may stir a memory or two from your own childhood.

As a little girl, I was curious about everything. My childhood adventures were spent almost exclusively doing two things—reading or exploring. Blissfully, I came of age in a world where the literal "wonder years" meant digging in the dirt, trying to sell crayfish from our creek to the neighbors, and whiling away hours in the giant lap of an ancient willow tree large enough to hold three kids under the age of 10. On cold and rainy days, my little sister and I commandeered the living room to create blanket forts, perfect for hunkering down with a stack of Nancy Drews and jigsaw puzzles.

Television was for evenings only, except for the occasional Saturday morning cartoon. But even TV was the stuff of adventure for me. Laura Ingalls came off the pages and onto the screen, and the raucous Walton children created in me a longing to live on a blue mountain in Virginia, running around in my bare feet and fishing in clear streams. Even now, when I think of these two shows, my first thoughts aren't of the people, but the places. Walton's Mountain and the prairies of the Midwest were the stars of the shows, and they created a yearning in me I wouldn't know to put a name to for years.

Other than a TV with four stations and a transistor

radio, I don't recall any entertaining electronics. I had a creek running through my front yard, lots of friends in the neighborhood, a bike, and a mom who would happily stick a pitcher of red Kool-Aid on the porch and send us off for the day. Life was good. We wore homemade clothes and short-cropped hair (easier for mom!), and I rarely recall eating out, unless the picnic table just off the back door counted. Big adventure meant a trip to the old Italian place in town, where baseball-sized meatballs were balanced atop a pile of spaghetti always served by an imposing old woman in a tight gray bun.

Is my childhood interesting? Probably not very. Unique? Hardly. Relatable? Maybe! Many kids growing up in or around small-town America in the 70s probably have similar tales. We worked diligently at school, did our homework, played flashlight tag, and prayed for a big snow. Not because that meant we didn't have school—I rarely remember a school-free snow day—but it made for great sled riding on the big hill across the street.

My childhood contains few real travel memories. But then again, no one I knew went very far. Not for vacation or any other reason. Sure, we had a station wagon that held all four of us and our collie, Mickey Mantle. My clearest memory of the station wagon (green with wood paneling—all the rage at the time) was getting my fingers smashed in the door. That's the stuff that sticks with you!

My recollections of childhood travel extend mostly to weekend trips to our beloved family farm, nestled in the mountains of north central Pennsylvania, 60 miles from home. Days there were spent swimming in the creek, fishing, riding on the wagon behind my Great Uncle Fred's ancient tractor, and desperately trying to catch and tame one of the wild cats that lived in the shed closest to the house. Sneaky devils. I don't think I ever actually put my grimy little hands on one, despite years of trying. Could be because the dilapidated shed, lit only by a bare bulb, was full of 100 years' worth of ancient junk. Everything from the old cider press to anything Uncle Fred didn't quite know what to do with. A treasure trove in itself (but it always scared me a little!).

Looking back, all of this contributed to the wonder I felt as a child. In my little world, I gravitated to anything that held mystery—anything that I could explore and hopefully figure out. There were time and space for my imagination to tumble ahead of me, to peer into the deep places. Beyond the cat shed, the bajillion sedimentary stones I turned over in the creek, always hoping to find a crayfish hiding in the murky swirl of water beneath. The thrill of "helping" Nancy Drew or Trixie Belden, and eventually Hercule Poirot, solve the case and catch the criminal. The sound a stone made when it was dropped into the mysterious rusty pipe protruding from the hill in our upper field at the farm—a left-over gas well from the distant past. Down, down, knocking into the sides as rock hit pipe until, miraculously and many seconds later, a definitive splash—certainly it was reaching Middle Earth. And always, forever and ever, the wonder of what might lie around the next bend on formerly untraveled road.

Big Wonder

Early on I memorized the names and route numbers of all the roads that carried us from our little ranch house to the family farm. My father loved maps, and he passed the obsession easily on to me. From my youngest fuzziest memories, I see the top of his full head of hair, eyes squinting through his glasses, peering intently at a map. I'm sure my desire to understand topography had as much to do with wanting his attention as it did deciphering the language of map-reading, but in either case I was all in. He patiently taught me the graphics of highways and back roads, how to calculate mileage, and that a main route ending in an odd number meant it traveled north/south, but an even one ran east/west. Somehow all this was equal parts fascinating and inspiring, even mysterious. I fantasized about transforming those lines and squiggles into actual adventures.

It was the summer I turned 12 that absolutely confirmed the connection between travel and wonder in my simple life, as our family of four prepared to drive cross-country to the unknown world of Wyoming. Mom and Dad packed the Chevy truck, and my sister and I found ourselves contentedly confined to the cap-covered back for three days with nothing but snacks and library books. Heaven. That summer, my passions for reading and exploring collided as we drove endlessly west on Interstate 80.

A singular moment on that trip would forever change how I feel about travel—a literal *take-my-breath-away* feeling. Our destination was Jackson Hole, Wyoming, and the Grand Tetons. When you're a scrawny little 12-year-old who's barely been anywhere, there's not much to prepare you for the first glimpse of an almost 14,000-foot snow-capped mountain. And I will remember that moment for the rest of my life. It's why I always liken the idea of wonder to coming around a bend, watching for what's on the other side.

One minute, we are driving across endlessly flat land, dying for the terrain to at least show a hint of the great peaks to come. Whether my memory is accurate or not is negotiable, but I recall everything being brown and flat for what seemed like days. And then, a curve in the road, and I'm face to face with the majesty of the Tetons, rising up from the floor of the valley into the clearest of blue skies, reaching for heaven. I had never seen anything like it unless you count Maria singing with the von Trapp children in the Alps. But somehow the view in person superseded the images of Austria on our fuzzy television.

That instant shifted how I looked at the world, and it is how I knew there was so much to explore. In that moment I realized that the world held unimaginable wonder that I knew nothing about, and I wanted to see it all. As a child, I didn't have the wherewithal to really know what that meant. Thankfully my childhood existed decades before we all carried the world in our pockets, so my "research" was courtesy of our World Book encyclopedias and library books. I marveled at the photos of faraway places and plants and animals I could only imagine. But the Tetons were my first up-close-and-personal moment with big wonder.

Real Life

Over the years to come, my world expanded slowly: a few car trips with my parents to New York City, Niagara Falls, North Carolina, Indiana, and Michigan, and my senior class trip to Florida, the latter the only one to fall under the umbrella of "adventure." (That particular week will forever live on in the memories of those who participated, and we continue to be thankful for the lack of social media.) College brought new friends and spring break trips, and I finally boarded a plane and took my first flight at about age 23. Two years later, marriage added the thrill of a honeymoon in Jamaica.

Grown-up life turned to the practical, overtaken happily and abundantly in the moment. Babies, house, school, jobs: the first bringing its own unique brand of wonder and the last three, all, deemed necessary and important. Essential. Life was good. And full! Adventure began to look more like a trip to the pumpkin patch with the kindergarten class or a soccer tournament or an evening out without kids where someone else cooked and did the dishes. Looking back, I wouldn't trade any of it for the whole wide world. The great passion for the unknown and travel took a literal back seat to life in that immediate present.

Wandering into Wonder

In the spring of 2003, though, my world grew exponentially. My closest friend had moved with her husband and children to Rome. I had never been across the pond but wanted badly to see this side of the world I had read so much about. My calling at that time was to be "mom," but the other hat I had worn most of my adult years was that of teacher. High school English and theatre teacher and then homeschool mom of two, I had always been fascinated with ancient Rome. This opportunity represented the ultimate field trip. Though it was hard at that time for me to spend ten days away from my own family, the idea of no responsibilities other than to soak up every blessed minute of my time in Italy definitely appealed.

I gleefully jetted across the Atlantic to spend ten days with my best pal. If you're a young mom, you can imagine the freeing feeling of sleeping and eating when you like and taking care of no other living thing. Once I got over the guilt—heaven! And in Rome! After the sleep of the jet lagged, we set off to walk through the heart of the old city. A seminal moment, burned in my brain . . .

We wandered along a side street near the famed Via Veneto. The day was balmy, with the yellows and pinks of spring tumbling out of boxes under windows older than America itself. Centuries-old warm ochre walls, slightly crumbling and radiating a welcome, watched over pedestrians picking their way along the cobbled streets. As we turned a corner and paused to admire pottery and housewares in a shop window, I was completely overcome. I just stood there and cried, feeling beyond foolish. Slightly weak in my knees, I recall saying, "I can't believe I am standing here."

Wonder had taken my breath away so completely, and tears of joy and gratitude came pouring out. It was unplanned and unexpected. It engaged all my senses. I had, in the most literal sense, wandered into wonder.

It was the Teton feeling—25 years later—that brilliance of pure and simple wonder that somehow was both small and large enough to stop me in my tracks. I basked in it, and then I knew I wanted more.

Travel as a Vehicle for Wonder

Dreams of travel, exploring the world, uncovering every secret hiding place to see the wonder beneath, behind, below—for most of my adult life this was not an active pursuit. My life was full, but of the other stuff, glorious and tragic in its own unique way. And then it wasn't. We all have a story. Kids grow up, life twists and turns in directions you don't see coming—there's life and death and loss. While some of it brings joy, there is inevitably heartbreak as well.

My story is a tale of all the above. I suddenly found myself alone for the first time in my adult life, save a few dogs. Life became something formerly unimagined. This wasn't what any of us had planned. Thankfully, my kids were now young independent adults and trying life on their own, but for my part, I needed a new blueprint. I will honor here that God knew the plan He had for me all along. He had my back, and none of it came as a surprise to Him who created not only the universe but every hair on my head.

It took me loads of patience to wait on Him as He revealed what I needed to know in His timing, and I gratefully credit Him for providing peace where there could have been continuing upheaval, and a sense of anticipation where anxiety may have remained. I trusted "in Him who is able to keep me from falling,"[4] and just put one foot in front of the other. But, still, at the outset . . . pain and loss, fear and uncertainty accompanied.

Shifting Forward

I believe that this is where instinct took over. The child of wonder, the young teen awed by mountain caps of snow 14,000 feet in the sky, the wife and mom reduced to tears on a cobbled side street on Quirinale Hill in Rome—she gathered herself together and knew, somehow, that the best first step forward was to fill up the gas tank and hit the road.

At the time, I couldn't have articulated why that response made so much sense. In truth I don't think I gave it a lot of deep thought. I just knew that going somewhere completely of my choosing and for as long as I was able was the next best step toward some sort of reclamation of the simple and the wondrous. It also guided me toward establishing firm footing in this new world.

For six weeks, I labored in love over maps and Google, planning a trip that was 50% whimsy and 50% plan. Six weeks of joy and anticipation, of figuring out how to sleep in my car because I couldn't afford a tent and hotels would be too expensive. Six weeks of highlighting road maps of half a dozen different states, researching the stories behind the little dots and tiny lettering representing small town after small town. I had no idea what I was looking for. I don't remember thinking I was looking for anything at all! I just so desperately wanted to go. And so, I did.

> *There is no exaggeration in the statement*
> *that it changed the course of my life.*
> *My life is still changing because of it.*
> *Somewhere over the course of*
> *those few weeks and 3,000 miles,*
> *life shifted forward.*

In the dust behind me, I left fear, uncertainty, and a lot of sadness. I found the beginnings of joy, purpose, and confidence. Actually, I discovered *me*. Not someone wholly new—just recovering and reclaiming significant parts of me that had been MIA for quite a while.

How did taking a solo road trip (not even a dog with me at the time) shift life forward? How could a few weeks of travel change my life? Please understand that no one thing happened, nor did I encounter a person whose words or presence transformed me. It wasn't a magical sunset in Florida or an encounter with a bear in the Blue Ridge. It wasn't a literal mountaintop spiritual experience with Jesus. None of the above, and yet all of the above and so much more. The answers will become more evident as we dig in further, and that clarity will help set you up for your own experience with wonder.

Coming of Age on the Road

The "coming of age" story has long been a favorite in America. Jem in *To Kill a Mockingbird*. Phineas from *A Separate Peace*. *The Catcher in the Rye, Huck Finn, Little Women*. It's a long and growing list. These novels typically focus on the young—a logical time of growth and change in life. But can't we "come of age" when we're older? Consider this definition:

Coming of age is the act of experiencing a definitive shift in one's perspective, a greater realization of one's place in the world, and a further understanding of how personal actions and reactions are integrally linked.

—Lysa Heslov

I love this. It directly speaks to the concept of seeking wonder and reclamation—of cementing our place in the world. Age is irrelevant! We all "come of age" throughout our lifetime. As long as we are breathing and growing, the possibility to "shift one's perspective" continues.

My road-tripping experiences provide a backdrop for my ongoing coming of age. You will have your own coming of age moments as you discover freedom and wonder on the road. The chapters ahead will supply you with all the ins and outs of planning, leading you to less stress and more wonder. Please know that your road-trip experiences will be nothing like mine. You probably wouldn't love my exact methods as much as you think you might, because I do it all my way when I'm on the road, and that's really not fun for anyone but me. Trust that you'll have both the confidence and the necessary tools to create your own unique and wonderful way. That's a significant part of what makes a solo road trip so unique!

In the coming chapter, your first mission will be to spend a bit of time reflecting as you take stock of your own heart and mind. An honest look back often moves us closer to discovering the future God has designed specifically and uniquely for each of us. Scary? Of course it is. But don't worry—I'll hold your hand if you need to feel steady! I also won't ask you to do anything without first giving you the tools to be successful. The goal is to equip you and empower you.

You *will* undoubtedly find your own wonder on the road, and I promise you will know it when it happens.

> **At the end of each of the next several chapters, I'll provide you with an opportunity to begin to brainstorm your own way forward. Please take time to reflect and jot down anything that resonates with you!**

I Wonder . . .

1. We've talked a lot in this chapter about the "wonder years" of youth. Do you have childhood memories that still create a sense of joy or awe as you remember them? Take a few moments to write out what brought you joy and how you experienced wonder as a child.

2. Do you have a memory or experience that came to mind when you read about my moment in the Tetons or on the streets of Rome?

    a. If so, describe it as best you can remember. How did it make you feel?

    b. If not, is there a place you wish to go or an experience you hope to have that would possibly elicit such a strong reaction?

3. Why do you long to recapture simple wonder in your own life?

Chapter 3

A Pause to Wonder *Why*

By now I hope you're beginning to picture yourself cruising down a beautiful back road, eyes wide open to the wonder all around you. It's exciting! But before you pack your bags, let's plan a little side excursion together, and know that while wonder remains at the heart of it all, we're taking a moment to shift from *wonder* the noun to *wonder* the verb. (Ok, stay with me here. In full disclosure, the English teacher in me comes roaring out here and there, and she's unstoppable.)

I wonder. You wonder. You get the idea? Let's add one more word as we dig deeper . . . wonder *why*. We're going to dive into this question and take time to wonder why a road trip appeals to you. Why embarking on an adventure and stretching yourself to see and do new things feels compelling and fascinating. To break it down to its simplest form, why the heck do you want to do this? How did you get here, to this place where you made the active choice to consider planning such an adventure? where you determined to pick up and read this book? Clearly something about taking a road trip appeals, draws you in.

Intentionally examine your motivations. You may learn something about yourself here and ultimately lay out a more fulfilling adventure if you can put words to it. Some will find this exercise child's play and super obvious. For others, it may seem daunting. Either way, the likelihood is that you haven't dwelled much on your motivations. To help you find your footing, consider how you can complete this seemingly simple sentence:

I want to take a solo road trip because _________.

Maybe you have a specific answer, maybe you have an entire list! If you currently cannot string three words together to explain your *why*, if it's just a feeling or even a calling you cannot explain, that's equally awesome. Leading up to my first solo road trip, I could not have clearly expressed to you why I wanted so badly to get in my car and go.

This isn't a test, and you don't need to have some beautifully crafted response, or any response at all, but it's worth taking time to consider. For now, we are going to take some time to wonder why together. To pose the question is simply a starting place. We'll spend the rest of this chapter digging into it all.

But why ask *why*? Why not just go? You certainly can. And I bet you'll have a grand time. But consider these three reasons why wondering *why* for a bit will enhance the experience for you.

- You'll be less likely to aimlessly wander and more apt to find wonder.

- A little focus can go a long way toward feeling both confident and at peace.

- Having a sense of your motivations will also encourage and empower you to persevere in the face of any adversity you may encounter. The unexpected will happen, and not all of it will be glorious. (Do not fear! Plenty of space will be devoted to helping you think through these potential potholes.)

Getting Started

I did not labor over my decision to embark on that first trip. I honestly don't recall thinking through it even a little bit, yet God was working to prepare me. At the time, I wasn't paying enough attention to notice! I didn't ask "why road trip?" and I don't remember anyone else asking me either, but I was taking blind baby steps in that direction.

I had reached an unexpected point in my life where somehow I knew that taking a solo trip was the next right thing to do. My life as I knew it had become unmoored—I was literally wandering through my days—but planning and executing a road trip moved me not only from restless uncertainty to a semblance of confidence and direction, but also helped me shift from wander to wonder. Digging back into my blog, I found I'd articulated this a bit in the following entry from that first summer I took to the road.

. . . I just wasn't sure what I was doing. As in, why was I doing all this? Was I looking for something? A place? A feeling? People? For weeks [ahead of the trip] I muddled along, mostly on my morning runs,

trying to work this out in my head. I determined that time would tell, and there was no rush. In fact, those words became some of the most important in the weeks leading up to my trip. Deep breaths. No rush. Time will tell.

—From "Home for the Night," July 2018

I really didn't know! As with many of the things that have happened to me in the last few years, I can now see God's hand preparing me for that first adventure. I can see in the rear view the little pieces of my life that fell into place that summer, all preparing me not only for that experience, but all that has grown out of it. Oddly enough, I had no fear. It honestly didn't even occur to me to be scared in any way. I just put it in His hands. My glass-half-full self trusted that He would reveal what I needed as I needed it. It was truly adventure of the highest order, and I couldn't wait to go.

I experienced so much on that first trip. So many "firsts" where I learned courage and confidence. I slept in my car on top of a mountain, had a stand-off with a very large bear on the Appalachian Trail, found contentment and even fun sitting by myself in an Italian restaurant in north Florida. I lost my debit card in Fernandina Beach (mailed back to me weeks later by a good Samaritan!) and found that I truly enjoyed hiking by myself. Some tiny victories, a few defeats (not with the bear, thank goodness), and big progress in relation to my life up to that point. I started my blog, *Just Being Bing*, and wrote about my experiences—discovering along the way that my solo trip resonated with so many other people. It really was the beginning of transformation.

My WHY

In hindsight, my first big road trip was inspired by four different desires. Yours may be entirely different, somewhat similar, or currently fall into the category of mystery.

1. A Strong Desire to Slow Down

For me slowing down means moving away from the tumult and busyness of the day-to-day and opening my eyes to really see what's around me. I frequently allow everyday noise to distract me from experiencing all that God has put in front of me. As my life was shifting into a new direction, I needed to create space where I could experience His Creation and His presence.

2. A Desire for Time and Space to Think

That meant being alone and decreasing the pace of life. I felt that being alone in my car was a much more fun (and less depressing!) place to be than sitting at home alone or trying to scratch out bigger chunks of time for myself in my normal environment.

3. A Desire to Experience New Things with My Eyes, My Ears, and My Mind

My instincts led me to travel to places I'd never seen before. Tiny towns, curious back roads, places I'd seen glimpses of in ads, settings from beloved stories. As I began planning, nose in both map and computer, the scribbled lists overran the notebook pages as I added parks and waterfalls, a "best ever" praline shop, and hometowns of favorite authors. I wanted to see, smell, taste, and hear it all.

4. A Desire to Navigate Traveling Solo

Another layer of "new" meant discovering how I would handle being completely by myself. I relished the idea of being alone—I'd not had that for decades. On the flip side, I would need to manage times of stress, fear, and apprehension without another person to lean on. I needed to learn that I could deal with my fears and prove to myself that I was up to the task—fully capable.

I wanted to stretch my boundaries—to get out of my own way, my normal space, my rut, and leave my familiar world behind both physically and mentally. There was this internal sense of something budding. I wanted to feed that and see if it would grow.

Seeking Out the Familiar

One further desire emerged and was a bit more clandestine, as I wasn't consciously aware of my need in this area! When I charted the course of my travels, I found I was unknowingly seeking places that in some way felt like home. Not in the literal sense of the brick and mortar where I live, but in that welcoming feeling of having come upon something I already know and love. A home of the heart. Places that felt relatable and comforting, like pulling on a favorite well-worn sweater on that first truly chilly fall day.

Often, I sought out small towns that felt somehow familiar. It seems clear now that in my post-trauma world I wanted to change things up without leaving my life as I knew it in the dust—to stretch myself with new adventures while also gravitating toward a semblance of comfort. Maybe a bit like a little girl who's too big to hide behind mom's skirts but takes the childhood blanket along just in case!

In the end, all of this added up to an adventure of both freedom and wonder. Ann Voskamp's marvelous quote from *One Thousand Gifts: A Dare to Live Fully Right Where You Are* sums up all the above in one beautiful sentence:

> *[I wanted to go] sleuthing for the glory that slows a life gloriously.*[1]

Yes. I was glory hunting. It took slowing down, eyes and heart open, to experience the new and the familiar. So worth the effort, and I'll never get enough.

Discovery

I realize now that traveling alone in your vehicle creates an unusual environment, as it provides a unique opportunity to look out as well as in. Hours of time, little to no interruptions, quiet if you want it. Traveling alone for a chunk of time inevitably causes you to slow down. And when you do, the world bursts into full color right in front of you. Yes, you'll see new things, but you'll also see *anew.* And it's intoxicating. You become secondary to all that's around you. You become an avid and engaged observer, and your own world, your own life, fades into the background. I can't help but liken the experience to that moment in the *Wizard of Oz* when Dorothy walks from her sepia-tinted Kansas bedroom into the technicolor dream of that world somewhere over the rainbow.

I arrived home from my maiden road trip having gained so much more than I was looking for. Driving solo had granted me uninterrupted time to peel back the layers of junk that had been piling up for years, covering up ME. I had so many roles in life—wife, mom, employee, volunteer, friend, daughter, sister, etc. All good things for the most part, but I had somehow gotten buried beneath it all. While my faith was unshaken, in many ways my identity had become a mystery to me. I had no idea how to define myself. Until I did.

Ironically, the fog began to clear as I focused on what was in front of me and not within me. I went days without talking to anyone I knew. I stayed off my phone. I relished the moments of deep joy as I marveled at the Creator putting His creative glory on display. I experienced His grace and peace and love as I spent time with Him. I found my identity day by day in relation to who I am in Him, as He generously revealed Himself around every bend. Ever so slowly, as I kept my focus on seeing anew, I rediscovered me. Not me as defined by any earthly relationship, by who I needed to be for anyone else, but rather simply as an unconditionally loved and forgiven image-bearer of God. And I was incredibly grateful. I was ready to move forward, ready to turn the page to a future embracing new choices and decisions.

Your Turn

Maybe for you it's not that deep or complicated. Or maybe all this provides a sense of assurance and excitement. Whatever your starting point, I share my story as an encouragement to you. In the end, I don't think there's a lot of magic in making a choice to go. You just know. If the thought of taking these next steps scares you, read on and acquaint yourself with all the tools provided to gain the confidence you need. And then, when you leave the familiar behind and venture into the unknown, you can eagerly anticipate what might be around each bend.

It's possible that freedom found on a road trip just might be the catalyst to help you move forward. Or to help you slow down. Or both. Maybe your life isn't currently undergoing a seismic shift, yet you feel a pull or a push to try something new, and a road trip just sounds right.

Running Away

One consideration we haven't really explored here regards the temptation or desire to run away. Not quite like when you're five and you grab your favorite stuffed animal and hide in the corner of the yard hoping mom misses you, but big girl running because life is just too darn hard. I haven't addressed this motivation up until now because it's unlike every other reason that you may consider embracing a road trip, and it's not one I endorse. To put it simply, the heart of my message involves *moving toward*, not *running from*.

"Nomadic Matt" Kepka, who writes extensively about solo travel, and primarily overseas travel, shared this on social media:

> *"Here's one thing about using travel to escape: your feelings come with you. They sew themselves into the nooks and crannies of your backpack and hang there like dead weight as you carry them from place to place. Travel doesn't solve your problems. It just moves them overseas."*

I've given this concept a lot of thought, especially as it

pertains to the idea of turning wandering into wonder. I think that I can make a case both to agree and disagree with Matt.

True, running away from your problems doesn't make them go away. They'll be right where you left them when you pull back into your driveway on the back end of your travels. All those attempts to simplify and clear your mind become increasingly difficult and maybe even a bit dishonest if you're just trying to run away. In the end, it has the effect of being a mere cover-up, a band-aid. The wound underneath may not actually heal, but fester. I'd also make a case for the fact that, unless you're a rockstar at denial, your struggles and issues will never be far from you, no matter what mountaintop you stand on or sunset you revel in.

However, if you're trying to reclaim your life, or redefine some pieces of it, making that escape may just be what you need to jump-start the process of taking back your life. A road trip can absolutely serve to help you break things down to the simplest common denominator. And I see that as a good thing. You can own the process and peel back the layers of accumulated mire slowly as you go. In the end, you may find you breathe easier, sleep more soundly, and have a new appreciation for all that you've experienced, not to mention a better understanding of yourself!

Embarking on a solo road trip can be just the thing to help you move forward. Come to a place of peace with why you want to do this and write it down. If you just don't have an answer, then trust your gut and press on. Trust that there is a reason, even if it hasn't yet been revealed.

Pack all the stuff you need. (Help with all that in the coming pages!) Just don't take too much baggage with you. Consider our earlier discussion about finding peace in your present and embracing the fog. Remember you can only experience what's directly in front of you—and that's enough! When you finally hit the road, you can anticipate that the fog will eventually clear, one moment of wonder at a time.

45

I Wonder . . .

So what about you? While you may not need any prompting, consider these questions if you'd like to dig a bit into your own motivations.

1. What about a road trip appeals to you?

2. What about it intrigues or inspires you?

These questions may help you zoom in further to help you identify your "why".

1. Do you crave time and space to just slow down?

2. Are you looking for something?

3. Are you lost?

4. Are you trying to peel back some layers of junk that have cluttered your life?

5. Do you need space to help make a big decision in your life?

6. Do you need to simplify life for a bit?

7. Are you trying to find YOU?

8. Is it pure adventure?

9. Are you an explorer at heart?

10. Are you running from something? Maybe you're running to something?

Earlier in the chapter I posed this question to you. Perhaps your perspective has shifted a bit now, or you are able to home in on it a bit more. Give it a try.

I want to take a road trip because __________.

"Clearing the Fog"

I . . . wasn't gone 5 minutes before I had the most satisfying sense of freedom. In hindsight, I think that's why I headed to the mountains first. Clear, clean, fresh. All concepts I needed to apply to shed the gunk of everyday life and recover the joy within.

And looking back now on the day itself, it was God-designed and perfect. I've been praying about this trip for a long time. I can't explain it except to say that I have been compelled to do this. I couldn't NOT do it. So, I knew that God would honor it and lead me where I needed to go, and protect me and stretch me along the way. Somehow as the sky fell and raindrops pelted my windshield as I drove through the gate of Shenandoah National Park, even that seemed just right. The forecast was for this to be the last day of the epic summer rains of the past 10 days, and I just trusted that by the time I got to the campsite, all would be dry-ish.

The whole day became a metaphor for the trip ahead. Fog everywhere, with glimpses of sky and, at the many overlooks, quick previews of far-off valleys and the occasional peeking-through of a shot of blue or a ray of honest-to-goodness sunshine. I felt so much peace as I drove slowly (because you can't go over 35 without driving over a cliff) around each bend, not knowing what I would find, but always expectant. Sometimes I could only see about 50 yards in front of me, but I trusted the road was there and that the fog would clear. And it did.

While I don't profess that God brought rain down on Skyline Drive just to teach me a thing or two, He did use it to get my attention. As excited as I was about beginning my trip, the fog and rain forced me to go slowly, and to think about every turn and every view. And yes, there were just glimpses of what was to come, but I could only see what I needed to see, and trust for the rest!

Chapter 4

An Affair of the Heart

As I consider this bridging of wondering *why* to the more practical *how*, it seems ironic that I am sitting just around the cove from the incredibly beautiful "Deception Pass" and its similarly named bridge. Nestled in the islands northwest of Seattle between Anacortes and Oak Harbor, Deception Pass is a strait of turbulent, showstopping blue-green water separating the northern Fidalgo Island from its southern neighbor, Whidbey Island. A two-span marvel built in 1935, Deception Pass Bridge towers 180 feet above the swirling waters below. It's magnificent.

Bridges provide us with safe passage from one solid spot to the next. Here at Deception Pass, tumult reigns below in the form of whirlpools and rolling eddies—fit only for the expert to navigate. For the rest of us, safety is found in the two-part steel and concrete spans almost 13 stories above, ferrying thousands of folks each day to the comfort of dry land.

Like the marvelous bridge at Deception Pass, this chapter

serves as a connector as we move on from exploring the gut-instinct and wonder-pursuit of "why" and cross to the necessary important terrain of "where, when, and how." This bridgework is essential preparation to ensure your entire experience is unique to you. It's a bit practical but mostly driven by your own wonder-dream and design. Let your heart be your guide. Don't hold back—no reality checks allowed for the next few pages. Holy grails and hopes only. I'll rein you back in down the road and in due time.

Heart Connections

In those early days of planning my first journey, I wasn't necessarily practical as I sketched it all out. My world had been turned on its head, and I just wanted to go. Reflecting now, I can see that pain and loss led me to plan a trip that was equal parts heart and head. Had I decided to take my initial solo road trip when life was less stormy, I'm not so sure I would have let my heart play so large a role, as I am such a planner by nature. The messiness of that vulnerable season turned into gift as I unwittingly pursued what touched my soul. So many times I have seen God not only use chaos for good, but show me, in the most literal way, how pursuing goodness and beauty naturally leads to Him.

It's time to tap into what makes you tick, what you value and love, and where you find meaning. Take your time in these pages, as they're rich with opportunity. Investment here ensures you'll be able to really see what's in front of you, and your ultimate itinerary will steer you toward the things that touch your soul.

These next two chapters serve as bridges to link your unique pursuit of wonder to purposeful planning. We're not leaving wonder behind, however. Definitely not! We will be taking our precious cargo *with* us. Don't forget all that you've read so far. You'll need it to reveal the marvels and miracles burrowed into all the coming how-tos. Wonder remains at the heart of every step we take. Always.

Signposts

As we drive down a road, through town, or across the country, we rely on the visual signposts before us. Which way? How far until the next town? Is that route heading north or south? Is it really 57 miles until the next rest area? We depend on these markers to provide accurate guidance. But what about the internal signs that help you decision-make *before* you go? I'm talking about the gut instincts, emotions, and heart-tugs that push and pull us toward meaningful places and experiences.

In my world, these are the inclinations that compel me to seek out a little hamlet in the Blue Ridge Mountains where one of my favorite authors sets her stories so vividly that I long to see it for myself. My instincts compel me to turn down a dirt road just because, or pop my head into an old library or bookstore. These moments are occasionally spontaneous, sometimes planned. The decisions are intuitive, drawing me as a moth to a flame.

But they are not random. They are woven into the singularity of me, and I've learned to listen. Your own internal proclivities are clues to help you navigate a trip that satisfies your soul. They are the signposts we are going to explore and probe for the rest of this chapter. Your only job is to be honest with yourself! There are no wrong answers. Just pay attention to what moves you. This current discovery is one of the heart.

Tears

In Taylor Sheridan's panoramic television series *Yellowstone*, the character of Beth Dutton may be one of the toughest, most hard-edged and intense women ever written for the small screen. She's a lot. To watch her is to both admire her incredible sass and fear her terrifying ruthlessness. Evidence of any soft side to Beth is rare. At the beginning of one episode, the magnificent beauty of the Montana mountains at sunset is on display as she, her cowboy husband, ranch-owning father, and others ride horseback to the crest of a hill and come face-to-face with all that golden evening light. It's spectacular. Much to her father's frustration, she offhandedly labels the scene "very pretty," and follows up with, "I don't find this beautiful, personally. Too big. Too much space to be beautiful, to comprehend it." Dad sighs, disgusted, and moves on, shaking his head. Like I said, she's a hard woman.

The following day, her husband Rip takes her on horseback into a meadow on her family's ranch that she's never seen before. Rip asks, "Is this more your kind of beautiful?" Climbing off her horse, Beth stands looking into the field and is overcome. Tears immediately well up in her normally hard and feisty eyes. She can't speak. Totally unexpected—the sight of this little meadow touches something deep inside of her. A remarkable moment that stands in contrast to 99% of the rest of Beth—a vivid, light-filled signpost, connected to her heart. For Beth, the meadow felt like the possibility of home, something she deeply desired to redefine from her childhood.[1] The emotion was immediate and unplanned.

We all have these moments when something moves us so completely that our physical bodies cannot hold the rushing tide inside. Our only response is the overflowing of our eyes. These instinctive drops of salted water are signposts to your own wonder experience, and they're different for each of us. Consider this question, posed by author Emily P. Freeman.

> *What touches your soul so deeply that it causes tears to come out?*[2]

This outpouring of emotion directly connects to an understanding of what brings about wonder in your life. Tears have a direct line to the heart and speak only truth. Emily P. Freeman goes on to suggest that "maybe our tears are tiny messengers, secret keepers of the most vulnerable kind, sent to deliver a most important message—*here is where your heart beats strong. Here is a hint to your design.*"[3]

Yes! Your brimming eyes carry messages to tell you— "Pay attention!" and "This is important!" Tears help remind us what is essential to each of us, what touches us, what breathes joy and life and so many other God-given gifts into us. Identifying what creates unbridled emotion is a surefire way to determine what you hold dear.

What hits you in that place where your eyes leak from wonder? Maybe a particularly poignant story or unexpected vista, a childhood memory or remarkable experience? Contemplate what energizes you, what transports you, what moves you or pulls you in. What brings you to tears. Not the sad variety. The more powerful kind—the ones that are Creator-generated and awe-filled.

Start here. Tears are a signpost of what is significant: what resonates with you and touches your soul. It may not be a place, but a person or an experience. Perhaps it's something from the past that hints at who you are and your place in the world. For some it may be a town, a building, a home. Or land where family once lived or where great grandparents walked and worked and breathed. Maybe what touches your soul relates to a childhood experience, or a great loss. It could be as personal as reuniting with someone meaningful in your life. If reading or movies are great loves, consider moments from favorite books, authors you relate to, movie scenes that resonate with you. Whatever it is, that innate rise of emotion is unique to you, and it's important.

If nothing comes to mind yet, skimming through a few experiences that touched my soul these past few years may help jump-start your imagination. While I planned many of the actual destinations, the moments that cause me to cry often take me unawares. In fact, I rarely see it coming, and then . . . eyes that sting with fierce joy and gratefulness. These unexpected episodes often lead to both wonder and tears.

Mansfield, Missouri – nostalgia and connection
An afternoon spent roaming the grounds of Laura Ingalls Wilder's home. I lived those books as a child. Laura was my friend and inspired me to so many of my own childhood adventures. Wandering the property where she lived with Almanzo and raised Rose was incredibly poignant for me. Seeing with my own eyes the room where she wrote was powerful and meaningful and inspired me in my own desire to share and storytell. The connection was immediate and a deep sense of familiarity swept over me as I found myself stepping into the space of the stories that had captured my imagination for so many years.

Gettysburg, Pennsylvania – appreciation

While I live close by and it's not exactly a road trip to wander the battlefield, Gettysburg never fails to touch something deep and strong inside of me. Lexi and I hike there often, walking the roads and trails, frequently encountering men and women who are on a pilgrimage to locate the spot where a family member fell wounded or gave his life, or to find the monument marking where his regiment fought during those bloody July days in 1863. Often, we end our day at Little Round Top, watching the sun set, turning the broken and storied fields below golden in the waning light. It feels like a wash of grace and mercy and forgiveness for all that happened there. The enormous sacrifice so many boys and men gave on those three July days remains palpable.

Cheney, Washington – joy

For over two decades, my closest friend has lived at least 3,000 miles away. A cross-country road trip to Washington State provided us much overdue time to be together—to spend time in her relatively new world as rancher's wife, sitting side by side on the dock of the lake below her home, feet dangling in the cool water. She and I are connected at the heart—past, present, and future—and it gave my heart overwhelming joy to be in the idyllic place her own contented heart calls home.

Charleston, South Carolina – connection

A long-ago day spent engrossed in maneuvering through the heart of the southernmost streets in the magnificent city of Charleston, South Carolina. Pat Conroy's beautiful novel *South of Broad* is a tale of friendship, family, and coming of age. Set against the backdrop of America's "Holy City," it remains one of my most treasured books. Conroy's attention to geographical accuracy always resonates with me, and I determined to trace the paper route of his protagonist, Leo, where he'd pitched newspapers at the homes of little old ladies and the town's most notable businessmen each morning. While no one would ever confuse me for a southerner, I have felt deep connection in my adult life to the Low Country of South Carolina and its magical jewel of a city.

Lonepine, Montana – grace

One summer Sunday morning, clear and bright with promise, I drove through ranch and farm land on the edges of western Montana, radio on, peaceful views on either side as I headed to Idaho and beyond. And then a song from deep in the archives of time, not heard for at least a decade, immediately reduced me to a puddle. Music has power. And the piano and the voice, together with the drive and the sunlight and the sense of well-being knowing to Whom I belong and that I am fully known, overwhelmed in the best way.

As you can likely tell, my personal signposts tend to revolve around beauty, but also connection—the something that touches memory and nostalgia or brings suddenly near people I love and admire. Vivid memory that transports me to pivotal moments in my own coming of age, some real and perhaps even some imagined. Each of these moments, and untold more during the course of each adventure, ties directly to what makes my eyes shine with gratitude for the opportunity to experience a moment of grateful wonder.

What about you? As you contemplate time on the road, consider what would bring you joy, what breaks through your barriers and scrapes you raw until you're just eyes brimming over with thanksgiving or peace or grace. Intentionally seek that which holds meaning for you. Your heart can be a tremendous guide for where to begin, to help you home in on what's important to you and unique to your world. In the wise words of Emily P. Freeman: "Listen to what makes you cry."

Treasure

We've considered what moves us, what draws us in and tugs at us—what brings tears. As we move step by step toward the inevitable practicalities, don't lose sight of these key signposts. Hold them close.

Tears are not, however, the only indication to point you toward wonder as you sketch out your unique adventure. While they are a surefire way to know if something touches your soul, paying attention to what you treasure also shines irrefutable light on what's important to your heart.

> For where your treasure is, there your heart will be also.
>
> Matthew 6:21

When we think about what we treasure, we are saying, "This is valuable to me. It is meaningful and worth protecting." We identify our treasures as essentials—of great value and highly prized. Chances are, your treasures are intrinsically connected to your heart, whether they be material or immaterial, tangible or intangible.

Your tangible treasures are easy to identify. People may likely top the list! And the touchstones. A grandmother's wedding ring, your child's baby photos, a rug bought during a once-in-a-lifetime trip to Turkey. The items you'd grab if the house were on fire and everyone was out safely. Those few treasures worth taking a risk to ensure their safe-keeping and that provide a continued visual memory that indicates meaning.

And what about treasures of the heart? Intangible valuables that make you stronger, wiser, content, complete. They are essential to your world—these ideas and ideals so worth protecting—what your heart values and longs for. As adults, and it seems to me especially as women, we often recognize their value in light of their absence. Perhaps it's the rejuvenating down time you currently do not have in your life but crave, or the breathing space you know you need to be at your best for yourself and for others, but pressure comes from all sides and there's no time for such things. It could also be the opposite—a new chapter of life where there is too much time, and you feel empty, lacking in purpose and joy.

There may be a palpable ache when you reflect on your intangible treasures. You know you need to find time to focus on something other than your messy everyday-ness. Or you are missing someone so much that if you can't go visit your heart just might shatter. Perhaps your explorer's heart needs to be filled with new sights and sounds.

These heart-longings look different to each of us. In my world, quiet time in the morning is one intangible treasure. Whether I am at home or traveling, I need those set-aside early moments for devotions, prayer, and time to settle my mind. It sets me up to be intentional about the day in front of me and keeps my focus on my Creator.

Take a moment to consider what you treasure.

- What fills you to overflowing?
- Are you currently keeping those cups full?
- What does your current day's pattern of demands

leave no room for? What curiosity or desire have you set aside because you haven't known how to make a place for it in your life?

- Could those desires be fulfilled as part of your road-tripping journey?

If the answer to the last question is even a possible yes, think through how time on a solo adventure may provide a fresh start in these areas.

Let's face it, the calls of the normal day-to-day often lead us to bypass and work around some of the treasures that make us better. Personally, I find it difficult to recognize the need for a "game-time adjustment" before I've dug myself a considerable hole. We push relentlessly forward, often because there's no alternative—it's just life! On the back side, however, we are left with empty tanks, and we crave a change of perspective. For most of us, this is where that burning desire for some type of getaway or vacation comes in.

When I made that first commitment to try a road trip, my proverbial tank was pretty empty. Admittedly the situation was unusual and one I never wish to repeat. In the space of less than a year, we sold what I thought was going to be our forever home, my husband of 26 years moved on to reconnect with his college girlfriend, and two of our dogs died. I had a confused daughter in college and an angry son at home, both trying to find their own footing in the world. Our identity, to some extent, was shaken. Brokenness in every direction. It was not a great year.

Five months later, I packed the car and determined to turn a page somehow. What did I treasure that summer? Well, I was holding on to Jesus with clenched hands—a good start! There was a sense of a blank slate, and it wasn't all scary.

I think I just drifted forward, somehow, toward the beginning of an unexpected phase of life. I craved solid footing for myself while trying to create that very thing for my kids. Past that, I longed for space. And time. While in some ways I had more of both than I'd experienced in a quarter century, I needed a fresh outlook and perspective. I wanted the opportunity to see new things and explore outside my own world which had collapsed inward in so many ways.

We travel because we need to, because distance and difference are the secret tonic to creativity. When we get home, home is still the same, but something in our minds has changed, and that changes everything.

—Jonah Lehrer

A journey can bring perspective, a rejuvenation of faith and hope, a place for peace. This may be a clue to why we feel this desire to get in the car and go. It's not that we want to run away, but that we need to see things differently. We crave the opportunity to see new things—to experience life anew. The going out with eyes and hearts wide open allows us to come back fresh and renewed.

Determining what you treasure and deliberately planning with those essentials in mind will help you figure out how to move forward. Like your tears, these treasure signposts tell you what you need, what is important to your heart and your mental health.

By no means exhaustive, consider this list of intangible treasures that your heart may crave but not always keep in stock.

Peace	Time	Adventure
Quiet	Space	Discovery
Faith	Joy	Connection
Freedom	Wonder	Relationship

Circle/write down all that apply. Please add your own! Take a little time to sit with the question and listen for your heart's answer. If your mind is too muddy for clarity to emerge, leave the deeper dive and immediately respond. It may be as simple as completing the sentence:

I treasure ______________________.

Does this mini exercise immediately create a list that ignites longing and recognition? If so, those are the untouchable, unfulfilled treasures currently sidelined in your world. They are signposts, pointing you toward what makes you whole.

Tears and treasures. While it may seem a little foggy for you now, I assure you you're well on the path to finding your way forward.

Passion

While tears flow out of a heart making connections to what matters, your dormant treasures sit piled up alongside, waiting to be called back into action. By now, you know a little more about what moves you, and you have a better handle on what you value. Time to investigate one other piece of your heart . . . passion.

No alarm clock needed. My passion wakes me.

—Eric Thomas, Ph.D.

You know that feeling, right? Emotion, fervor, longing, even zeal. The *Britannica Dictionary* defines passion as "a strong feeling of enthusiasm or excitement for something or about doing something." Chances are, something that qualifies as passion in your world comes quickly to mind.

Passions are personal. They play a role in defining each of us as we tend to devote time and energy to that which we feel passionate about. Quite often passions are obvious. Think about five people you know well. I bet it isn't too difficult to name at least one thing each is passionate about. Know any Argentine or Brazilian soccer fans? That's passion of the most intense and undeniable variety. Those folks are crazy about their fútbol. Many of us may not wear our passions so clearly, but the fervor is no less intense in our hearts and minds.

For some of us, the things we feel most strongly about may not be reflected in how we currently spend our time. Our "regular" life has claimed our attention and we've put our burning desires to one side, hoping to come back when we're older, when things settle down, when we can afford it. Whether your passions play a meaningful role in your every day or they still live in the land of "someday," use this moment to take stock.

Consider what drives you, interests you deeply, makes you sit up and pay attention, or causes you to stop scrolling. Is it a philanthropic cause? A sport team? A hobby? A deep desire to serve others or learn something new? Is there something you dream of doing? And the obvious one since you're reading this book—are you passionate about travel?

As we head closer to the point where you determine the details of your own road trip, pay attention to your passions.

Incorporate something about what drives you and excites you into your planning. It will go a long way toward ensuring you find yourself face-to-face with wonder.

Putting a name to your passions will also help you plan. It likely will drive your decisions not only regarding *where* you go but also *how* you organize your experience. In fact, even if you struggle to identify those passions, your decision-making as you plan will likely cause them to bubble to the surface anyway. Keep in mind that what drives you and ignites you as you move forward could be something you've thought about for years. Alternatively, a completely new excitement may have taken hold of you recently, especially if you are in the midst of some significant life changes and part of your thinking is to get out of your rut or comfort zone.

I'll prompt you more specifically at the end of the chapter, but for now, complete this thought as best you can:

I am passionate about _______________________.

On the chance that examples help, these two passions surfaced and have now prevailed in this chapter of my life:

- I instinctively feel pulled toward intense beauty and seeing the glory of God in His creation. I have an intense longing to see as much of the natural splendor of our country as possible.

- I am deeply drawn to the feeling of belonging and connection—to find places that feel like home.

That first summer my life felt somewhat rudderless, and no doubt I was searching. I sought out small towns in rural America that felt welcoming and "homey." Wondering my way around charming southern villages that summer, admiring quaint old homes with lovely front porches, fulfilled the passion to dream about where I might belong.

After many subsequent journeys all over the US, my approach to travel hasn't changed. I know what fuels me, and I know what's important to my heart. Any travel I take pays heed to these passions. Keeping them close ensures that my eyes will be open to God's leading.

Fully embracing and understanding my passions, tears, and treasures has been transformational outside of my road-tripping experiences as well. Once I understood my signposts, it became easier to start anew. The result? The purchase of a little Civil War–era home in a small town, with family, friends, and church nearby and endless beauty in my own backyard and in the hills and valleys beyond. I now enjoy the incredible gift of sharing my passion with others through my business and, now, this book. I learned to listen to what makes me cry, paid attention to what I love and what fills my soul to overflowing. Whether I am at home or on the road, everything I need is right here with me.

Putting It All Together

As you lean into your heart's leading, chances are you'll discover that your treasures, your passions, and what makes you cry bear some similarities. Mine are intrinsically connected. The beauty and glory of God's creation pair with my desire to experience places and people who resonate with me. Add to that the gift of time and peace and a very intentional slow pace so I don't miss anything. All of these become integral pieces both of the planning phase and the spontaneous decisions I make along the way.

When you lead this whole process with your heart, the

rewards can be magical. Knowing what resonates with you primes you for eyes-wide-open adventure. It's fulfilling, joyful, hopeful. Each day before putting the car in drive, I pray what has become my consummate road-trip plea—that God would keep my eyes wide open to all He wants me to see and experience each day. I don't want to miss anything He has for me!

While you are likely creeping toward identifying your own signposts, you may not yet see how that information will directly carry over to the journey itself. I promise you, it will. Consider, though, that it will likely be more process than checklist, and there's no firm deadline. It takes time—time to think, pray, and ponder. Time for sweet and slow revelation. Time to work through the questions already posed and the plans in the chapters ahead. These signposts are the first pieces in building a way forward to an adventure uniquely and wonderfully yours.

I Wonder . . .

This chapter provides us with an opportunity to pause and consider what we hold dear and will help set you up to make decisions about your travel that will meet your unique heart-needs. Take a few moments and think about each question below.

1. What types of situations, places, experiences, etc. make you cry with an excess of joy, wonder, or awe?

2. Reflect back to the intangible treasures shared earlier in the chapter. Which ones do you relate to?

3. Complete this sentence with as many responses as apply: I am passionate about _______________.

4. Earlier in the chapter, I mentioned that my first trip was planned with "equal parts heart and head." What about you? We will explore this tension thoroughly when we dig into planning, but give it some thought now. Are you more likely to be a practical planner, or one who follows her heart for each decision?

Journaling option: Write a paragraph or more and envision your own road trip. What would bring you joy in your journey?

Chapter 5

The Treasure Map

Spring fever. In my house, the passage into warm breezes and unending yardwork coincides with the joyful season of maps spread over the dining room table. My laptop and assorted scraps of notes sit to one side, new composition book splayed open, highlighters and pencils at the ready to make note of all the thoughts and brainstorms.

Over the long winter and early spring, I have tucked away all the little inspirations and ideas that have crossed my path—they come to me through books, movies, Instagram posts, over coffee with friends. Some find their way into note form on my phone, others onto slips of paper, saved social media posts, as Pinterest boards or scrawls in my adventure notebook. Still more roam around untethered in my head. It's time to bring them out into the light of day to weigh fascination against possibility.

Each snippet and fragment of idea relates to my passions, what I treasure, what brings me joy. All these crumbs are tied to my version of wonder. There's no checklist of approval to make the cut. The process is innate and the notion wouldn't be there unless it connected inherently to what I love. No thinking required. In the end, I know what I love and I know what I don't. Chances are you do too!

This is really the starting gate for wonderous adventure. This magical connection between my heart and the tangible, touchable, seeable reality, and it all begins with those heart-guides, those signposts:

- **Tears:** what moves me?
- **Treasures:** what fills my need for peace and space, and for satisfying my constant curiosity?
- **Passion:** what do I long to see, to experience?

My jumbled snatches of ideas will inevitably need to be winnowed down, as there are far too many points of light for one adventure, no matter how long or how grand. But for now, I pour it all out there, ready to transform into a veritable treasure map, full of possibility and wonder.

A short time-out here for those who feel rising anxiety about taking a long trip. After examining your current state of affairs, you may know a lengthy trip is just not feasible. That's okay! You can still tap into the excitement of possibility and create a treasure map that works for your situation. Your adventures may begin as a single day or two, or a long weekend. Just because your road trip is shorter doesn't mean it will lack joy, wonder, and freedom. If this likely describes your first wonder journey, there is an entire chapter up ahead, devoted entirely to those who need to dream in smaller chunks of time and space.

It's Your Move

Wherever you are, be all there. —Jim Elliot

Jim Elliot's words provide the perfect sentiment for this juncture in our search for wonder. This is what we long for, to uncover those moments and places that take our breath briefly from our bodies, capturing every fragment of our imagination and attention. These moments when God reveals His creation as so much joy. These are the moments to be "all there."

I think of this quote when I'm planning and when I'm on the road. Much like the lyrics from "Keep Me in the Moment," it reminds me to be fully present as I travel. I consciously plan to leave distraction in the driveway at home, ensuring that while I'm on the road, I can be "all there."

Now, it's your time. Time to create your own unique-to-you, one-of-a-kind treasure map to wonder, to dream and imagine all the places where you want to arrive and "be all there." Time to take your guideposts and begin to match them up with tangible, touchable scenes and places that hold meaning for you and draw you in.

You may already have a solid idea of what some of those places and experiences are—you know what intrigues you, draws you in, brings you peace, and fills your passion bucket. At the very least you probably have an inkling by now. Maybe you've been carefully stashing your own travel dreams away, waiting for the time to bring them out to play.

If you can't quite imagine how to get out of the starting gate, this is hardly discouraging news! I envy you a bit in that your slate is blank and anything is possible. This chapter will provide the beginnings of even more adventure for you.

Dreams for Days and Decades

It's time to bring our signposts to life, put skin and bones on them, connect our passions, tears, and treasures to experiences you can see and touch and smell. What do those feelings and emotions look like in your world? The sky is truly the limit for the moment. It's time to connect your passion to place as best you can. Think about what you treasure. I guarantee there are plenty of unique and interesting locations, people, and adventures that will speak to the longings of your heart.

Treat these next moments as a written exercise based solely on your instincts. We all have places, people, and experiences we dream of visiting. Take a few moments and name the ones that immediately come to mind. Don't hold back. Don't concern yourself with the details of distance, potential cost, or time. Don't stress about specifics. We'll get there eventually. For now, just dream it all out and write it all down.

This list is the instinctual manifestation of your passions, spirit-brimming tears, and treasures. Your list is uniquely yours. God's unfathomable attention and care to the calls of each of our hearts amazes me. He knows every hair on your head, and He knows what makes you weep in awestruck wonder. As you step into embracing your passions, what a freeing feeling to know that your Creator is calling you to go forward and explore the beauty and glory He has created for you. I hope you can see the wonder in that!

Mining for Ideas

If your list isn't coming easily, take a deep breath. This isn't a timed assignment, or a test of any kind! This is you, pondering what your heart looks like transformed onto a map. It will take some time, and, with practice, it will become an ongoing exercise for years to come.

There are many ways to give this process a kickstart. These next few sections will lead you toward what inspires you, and provide you with a little prompting before you take off scribbling into the night. If you're already well on your way—amazing! I'm betting there is more inspiration to be mined as you read on. Keep that pen in hand as you continue to uncover what resonates with you. Remember that the goal for now is to compile places and adventures that excite you, connect to your signposts, and make you consider jumping in the car right now! Research will play a role for sure, but not yet. Just dream.

As I sit at my desk just now, I am surrounded by no fewer than seven books, three composition books, and at least three maps scattered within inches of me. And none of them are actual references for my writing. Nope. The notebooks are filled with ideas of dreamy locations and stops for upcoming trips, the maps (I have a bit of an addiction here) provide opportunity to visualize and navigate my wonderings, and the composition books, not to mention legal pads and sticky notes, all play a role in the adventures to come. I am rarely at a shortage for places to explore. I venture to say that before long you won't be operating at a deficit either.

But where do these ideas originate? Each of the following proves to be an unending wellspring of inspiration for me, though there are plenty of other places to experience that spark of wonder as well. See what resonates with you.

Novels

This is a big one for me. It's no secret that I am drawn to connections with people and places, and I love finding those connections in novels. One of my most beloved authors, Jan Karon, writes beautiful novels set almost exclusively in her created mountain town of Mitford, North Carolina. I've driven the roads of that region, visited towns and hamlets in the area, always on the lookout for those same views her protagonist Father Tim enjoys while on his morning runs with his Great Dane, Barnabus.

Travelogues

In addition to novels, travelogues inspire me. This genre runs the gamut, from the beautifully written to the not-so-much. They're personal, and inevitably take the reader along for the ride as the authors discover more about themselves and their relationship to what they encounter along the way. I am currently knee-deep into the travels of Alice Steinbach as she left behind her journalism career at the Baltimore Sun for nine months of exploration in Europe. My wonderlists for France and England have become considerably longer as I travel with Alice.

Social Media

Ugh. I hesitate to say much here as it is such a slippery slope, but there are wonderful ideas to be mined in this space! I tend to follow people who enjoy traveling the way I do, or who go to places I find interesting. I do a lot of saving and pinning to Pinterest so I can come back later.

Documentaries

I love American history, so often I am drawn to historians like Ken Burns, who have done all the hard work of discovery, allowing me to sit back and soak it all in. Burns's documentary *Lewis & Clark: The Journey of the Corps of Discovery* captured my imagination a few years ago and played a role in determining pieces of my itinerary into the Pacific Northwest. A memorable moment that summer found me standing on a hill near Astoria, Oregon, a few miles from the Pacific. Merriweather Lewis and William Clark stood on that same ground in 1805, finally gazing upon the ocean 18 months into their amazing expedition. Eerie and cool.

Television and Movies

Of course! Who can resist wanting to head west after watching *A River Runs Through It* or dreaming of catching a flight to seek out Highclere Castle of *Downton Abbey* fame? Maybe cities are more your thing, and you loved the vibe of New York portrayed in *When Harry Met Sally* or *Seinfeld*. And don't be shy about your viewing habits—reality shows like *The Amazing Race* or *The Bachelor* or *Bachelorette* can easily inspire a desire to explore unique locales. A few years ago, I determined my summer road-trip destination based solely on the beautiful landscape in the Netflix series *Virgin River*!

Other wonderful inspirations are found in television shows and series devoted to travel. Not to mention the entire

Travel Channel! Many of these focus on overseas travel, but there are wonderful American options as well.

Friends and Family

While this may sound obvious, I'm always amazed at the variety of ways ideas pop up through friends and family. Photos of travels seen on Facebook or Instagram, conversation over coffee talking about where so-and-so went or asking "have I heard of?" or "have I seen?" and the inevitable discussions where we are just dreaming about places we'd like to go.

Where Roads Diverge

American poet Robert Frost has been encouraging us for just over a hundred years now to take "the road less traveled." I often return to this sentiment when considering an area of the country to investigate, thinking back to when I may have traveled quickly through some place as a child or with other people, wishing I could stop and stay awhile or get off the main road to see the sights. From the time I was in college, I annually drove south on Route 95 with friends or family heading for a week or two of warm sand and blue water. The goal was always to get there as quickly as possible. No regrets, and I still do it occasionally! But what about all those places to the east and west of the necessary nightmare of I95? Several years ago, I decided to investigate and found whole other worlds in northern Florida, Georgia, and South Carolina.

Additional Sources

Over the years, I've also drawn inspiration from magazine articles, even news stories and commercials. Alternatively, diving into search engine results on Google, YouTube, etc.

tends to muddy the waters for me and prevent me from focusing on what makes my heart glad. I inevitably get dragged into the "Top Ten" lists of absolutely everything and everywhere, far from any focus on my own signposts.

Casting the wide Google net does have its role, and you'll be glad to have it at your disposal a bit later on! Your current intention, though, is to envision places that fit your wonder-profile, not to engage in wide-ranging brainstorming research.

Take a few moments to think through what some of these suggestions may have triggered in your memory. Consider what you have read, watched, heard, and been drawn to over time, and add them to your growing list of ideas!

Adventure Ideas

What about all those dreams you've been stockpiling over the years? Consider places you've always wanted to go, people you'd love to visit, events that excite you. How about the balloon festival in Albuquerque? Childhood friend in Texas? Sunrise in Sedona? Wrapping your arms around a redwood tree? Attending the Little League World Series? Maybe you've always imagined visiting the tulip fields in Washington or experiencing Hemingway's Key West. Whatever you've wished for, write it down!

Take a Walk on the Wild Side

Now's a good time to consider dreaming some daring dreams as well. Want to jump out of a perfectly good airplane? Bungee jump the New River Gorge in West Virginia? White water raft Wyoming's Snake River? Maybe you'd like to ride a dogsled or hike a volcano. Let me add an unlikely one to the list: Attend a rattlesnake hunt? If so, there's an infamous one in Potter County, Pennsylvania, I can refer you to. Honest.

Festivals

Another endless avenue of possibilities includes seeking out festivals, celebrations, and locations that are centered around something you love or enjoy as a hobby. Some are famous within their circle of followers, like perhaps a Fungus Fest. Yes! If you love your mushrooms, you can find quite a few variations on this theme throughout the country! There are garlic festivals, pillow fight events, and duct tape festivals. Just about anything you're into likely has a festival connected to it! My personal favorite involves Phil, the world-famous prognosticating ground hog in Punxsutawney, PA. If you're a bit of a risk taker, or just want to see something weird, add a festival to your list and get out there and claim it!

Bucket Lists

Maybe your passions lead you toward bucket list–type experiences. Go for it! How about a few days to experience shows on the Las Vegas Strip or soak in the enormity and eclectic beauty of New York's Central Park? Maybe driving through the Redwood Forest appeals or jamming to jazz on Bourbon Street in New Orleans. Alternatively, a trip to the Macy's Parade for Thanksgiving or Times Square for New Year's might excite you. On the opposite coast there's the Rose Bowl Parade or perhaps a Superbowl. The options are unending.

The Long and Winding Roads

Perhaps driving a particular route fits your style better. Thousands of road-trippers seek out all or portions of the fabled Route 66 each year, venturing from Chicago to Santa Monica, California. Full of quirky stops along the way, it makes for an amazing adventure. One summer, as part of a larger trip, I spent three days driving most of Florida's A1A, the coastal road that begins in the Keys and mimics the Atlantic coastline all the way to Fernandina Beach, the Sunshine State's most northern coastal town. Amazing. Looking for more dramatic seascapes? The Pacific Coast Highway might just be the ticket. It all comes back to those treasures and passions.

Small Dreams

If all of this seems over the top (you may be a simple girl, after all!), then dream small. It's *your* dream, and you know what you treasure, what makes your heart beat strong. To be honest, small is more my wheelhouse. Visiting lavender fields in western Washington or walking the streets of small southern towns in search of ice cream, chasing waterfalls in upstate New York, sipping wine at a vineyard in the Shenandoah—that's more my style. These are the things that speak wonder to me. Maybe they're yours too. Whatever it is—go for it. Give it a name and write it down.

An aside to address those of you who are pleasers, who find yourselves making decisions based on other's expectations. I am a total work in progress in this area myself. That is why I need to tell my kindred pleasers this: This is a freedom adventure, and this is your list. You don't need to go to the Grand Canyon or see a Broadway show because everyone else does, or because others think you should. Dream your own dreams. You have full permission to remove all those "must see" places from your dream list unless they rightly belong on your personal treasure map.

Themes

In preparation for writing this book, I interviewed several other road-tripping friends and acquaintances to learn more about how they plan, what they love, what they don't, etc. It was no surprise that each person's experience was unlike any other! One approach that repeatedly popped up revolved around the idea of theme travel. Not theme *park* travel, though that could work too!

I found the topic fascinating, partly because I do not travel this way, and because, within the small group of people interviewed, each of those who engaged in "theme travel" went about it so differently from one another. In every case, however, the concept of a themed road trip informed their choices from the beginning of the brainstorming process.

It all comes back to what you love—what is meaningful. (Those signposts again!) There may be an easy connection between your passion and a theme trip. Maybe you love national parks, beaches or lighthouses, baseball or football. You can absolutely create a compelling list of possibilities from big broad themes like those.

Your passion may lead you to an entirely different interpretation of theme. You want to track down famous pizza places or the best coffee in Seattle. Some adventurers have a particular penchant for wineries, pottery, or city parks. No matter what tactic you take, seek out what you love, what inspires you.

At this juncture your mind may be reeling with possibilities and excitement. As your piles grow and your notes abound, don't worry if it seems you have too much! (That's never a thing.) We will work through narrowing down what you'll do for this first trip so that you can confidently embrace your plan. Many of your brainstorms will simply be set aside for other adventures. One of the spectacular discoveries about road-tripping is that you never ever run out of options, and your collection will make the next trip you take that much easier to plan.

My personal lists and ideas seem endless, and I can get overwhelmed with the sheer volume of places I want to spend time, visit, soak in. There's just SO MUCH. How in the world to make sense of all these ideas, put them in some sort of order or at least wrap my brain around all the possibilities? The solution is fairly simple. It's time to create your treasure map.

Creating Your Treasure Map

Before we rein in all our ideas, a word or two about maps. I'm super visual and an unapologetic map lover. Even if you're not, it may be helpful to begin with a big ole map of the United States. While I use online maps for plenty of things, when it comes to big-picture dreaming and planning, I'm all about spreading the paper out on the table, or even hanging it on the wall. I want to be able to see it all at once.

We'll talk in depth about resources down the road, but if you're not currently in possession of a quality US map, you'll find a link for my favorite in the resources: <u>www.wonderbingtravel.com/book-resources</u> As you get further into your planning, having a US map where you can see the states in their entirety will help you navigate realistic expectations in terms of length and distance of travel.

If you plan to road trip in shorter, smaller chunks, be sure to purchase maps of your own state and any adjoining ones where you may choose to wonder. Each individual state map provides so much detail not available on a national map. I prefer to have both! I have a map for every state where I travel, but often refer to the entirety of the United States map to get the big picture of a long trip.

Once you've created and compiled your list of ideas, spread out your map and put a pin in each spot that calls to you. Highlight them, draw a heart – whatever works for you! It will help you get organized later, and for the moment it provides a visual connection between your passions and the places you'll find them.

Transforming my internal passions and treasures into physical form and watching them take shape on the map like so many little points of light inevitably fuels my wonder senses. You may be surprised by your own results! They will likely provide hints to how you move forward in your planning. Without this big picture of what you're drawn to, it's easy to become overwhelmed and discouraged, but seeing it all spread out before you may begin to unlock some of the mysteries of choosing a direction to point your car on Day One.

No Destination or Destination Known?

The scrawls and scribbles, highlights and hearts on my map radiate with the promise of treasure. I can't walk by it without pausing for a peek or to add another pin. But what is it telling me? How do I make sense of it all and settle on the wonders I'm being led to this time around?

Many factors go into this decision, and the next several chapters will delve into refining the plan. Before you start worrying about your bank account and timeline, or who's going to feed your cat, there is one other "big picture" item to consider . . .

Do you have a primary destination? Thinking back to my first big solo road trip, I inherently knew I needed a landing place to help me bookend the entire adventure. Being somewhat uncertain how the whole thing was going to go, knowing I was headed somewhere specific to rest and refuel before I returned provided me with a sense of peace and a bit of control (whether real or imagined!). I had considered a more roundabout trip, one where I didn't really "end up" anywhere, but it just felt wrong to me. Knowing there was a safe haven of sorts at my furthest point from home gave me both confidence and a bit of added security.

I've also learned that part of my success on the road means including a few solid touchpoints along the way—visiting people I know or settling down somewhere for several days to rest and enjoy a particular place on my own. That first year, I determined to land in Islamorada in the Florida Keys to visit friends. I planned to stay for a few days and then head back north, exploring a different route in the direction of home. Determining that piece from the beginning helped frame everything else more easily, provided me with one solid decision at the outset of my adventure, and inspired a bit of needed confidence!

In subsequent wonder seeking, I have fallen into similar patterns, no matter how long the trip. Depending on the length and distance of my travel, I may have multiple "destinations" along the way, staying for a few days with friends, renting an Airbnb, or calling a campground home for a few days. These landing spots offer me time to relax, park the car for a few days, do laundry and eat normal meals. I know what works for me (and for Lexi the Golden), and I plan accordingly. This gives me the best of both worlds—spontaneity on the road to explore to my heart's content with a planned respite or two before I gear up again.

Maybe you purchased this guide because you already had a destination in mind and just needed help with the rest. Congratulations and well done! If not, take some time to think about what approach may appeal to you. Would it be helpful to create a midway point where you can stay and rest for a while? Or perhaps, after considering all the dots on your map, a more circuitous route with no real destination makes more sense. It could also be that your passion is to drive a certain route from start to finish. If that's the case, then perhaps "the end" of that ribbon of road provides your destination before you turn around and come home.

If all you know is that you want to get in the car and go somewhere or the answer to the destination question seems too heavy to manage at this point, you can lay that burden down. It will all become clear as you move forward. Your eventual path and timeline to wander through the details is uniquely yours, and you will discover it organically as we go.

For those considering throwing all thoughts of landing spots to the wind, this next bit will speak to you. In his *Blue Highways* travelogue, William Least Heat-Moon truly captures the spirit of "just going." He had no intended *where*. For him, the not knowing *was* the story, and we live vicariously through him as he traverses America's back road for three months and 13,000 miles.

He begins his journey here:

I turned south onto state 45, a shortcut to I-64. After that, the 42,500 miles of straight and wide could lead to hell for all I cared; I was going to stay on the three million miles of bent and narrow rural American two-lane, the roads to Podunk and Toonerville. In the sticks, the boondocks, the burgs, backwaters, jerkwaters, the wide-spots-in-the-road, the don't-blink-or-you'll-miss-it towns. Into those places where you say, "My god! What if you lived here!" The Middle of Nowhere.[1]

Here was a man who had no plan—at a crossroads in his life after losing his job and separating from his wife—and no destination, approaching each new day with an open hand. While I have learned that what works for me doesn't quite parallel Mr. Least Heat-Moon's approach, I completely connect with his search for wonder via the back roads of America. We have both encountered joy there. Life for a 38-year-old man in 1978 looks a bit different than it does for you and me, and I'm not advising you take his path. There is, however, much to learn from the idea of "just going," not the least of which is discovering wonder in the wandering.

Dig into where your own passions and treasures lead you and draw you in—those places and enticements you can't let go. Name them, pin them, and repeat until you have a fist full of ideas or a map full of dreams. You're getting closer to real encounters with wonder in your soul.

I Wonder . . .

Before you move on, add any additional destinations or
dream spots to your map and lists!

Chapter 6

Going Solo

As a child, travel began and ended in the backseat of our giant station wagon, younger sister alongside and Dad and Mom up front. During the carefree college years and into my early 20s, my friends became my companions of choice. After marriage and children, most vacations were taken as a family. Our trips ranged from the packed-to-bursting mini-van beach weeks to the rare getaway with the hubby. The memories of these chapters bring smiles and happy thoughts, and I have been blessed with plenty of opportunities to explore near and far. But traveling on my own has proven to be an entirely different sort of adventure.

In my early 20s, I managed a handful of solo road trips to visit friends, but the travel was limited to getting from A to B as swiftly as possible because the destination was the fun! In those few independent years, I had little money and, usually, limited days before I needed to return to work.

The allure of going solo didn't hit until it wasn't an option.

As a young mom, the old 1970s catchphrase "Calgon, take me away" became something I could relate to! Of course, most days I would have settled for five minutes alone in the kitchen to eat ice cream out of the box in silence. Not much time to even daydream about solo travel, let alone consider it as possibility.

Finding Freedom on the Road

However, when my kids were 12 and 14, I found myself hitting the road alone for the first time in my mom memory, heading south to rural-ish Tennessee to pick up my daughter from church youth camp. Almost 8 hours of driving time and an overnight all to myself! The prospect loomed large and inviting. I remember the thrill of adventure as I set out, though I didn't stray far from the interstate the entire way from Northern Virginia to Knoxville.

The journey felt like freedom, and I instinctively pursued some wonder along the way. I found it in the form of the General Francis Marion Hotel in the tiny town of Marion, Virginia. Built in 1927, the old landmark had fallen into disrepair late in the 20th century until a local family resurrected it to its former glory in 2006. I can't quite find the words to describe how it felt to have one night in this beautiful, cozy hotel with its birdcage elevator and my very own charming giant door key. ALL BY MYSELF.

Eight years later, I sought out this charming spot again, this time on my inaugural two-week solo road trip. It didn't disappoint—just as cozy, familiar, and unique as before, it somehow felt like a proper sendoff and part of the larger adventure. A tangible, lovely confirmation that I was literally headed in the right direction, and on the road to wonder.

It's Your Time

The idea of solo travel certainly isn't novel, but for the masses, and for women, it is a fairly recent phenomenon. In the last decade alone, solo female travel has increased by epic proportions.

Between 2018 and 2019, the number of pins for "solo female travel" rose 350% on Pinterest, and in 2017, Google searches on the topic increased by 52% over the previous year. It's encouraging to see such a significant spike in this unique demographic, though interesting to note that 47% of women who embarked on a solo adventure fell into the 25-39 age bracket.[1]

While the stats perhaps suggest that my generation is missing the proverbial boat (or SUV, RV, minivan), I think there is a huge opportunity for mature women to embrace the joy and wonder of solo travel. Let's face it—most of us were not considering heading anywhere on our own in our later 20s and 30s. We were raising families, working, and supporting those around us in every conceivable way.

But gals like you and me are all grown up now, and solo travel is not just for the spunky millennial. In fact, it makes a world of sense that the women of the Gen Z and Boomer generations are much better equipped to embark on travels of our own compared to our younger counterparts. Until recently, though, the time may not have been right. Finances, careers, caring for children, attending to aging parents, spending time with spouses—all of these have trumped thoughts of solo adventure. But now . . . the kids are grown, the career is in the rear view or shifting, responsibilities are fewer in general. The timing is suddenly better than ever before.

If you fall into this beautifully "seasoned" age bracket, this may all sound great in theory, but you may worry that the years have left their mark, added other weight. (No, not that kind, but I feel ya in both the areas of unwanted marks and pounds!) Surely there was joy in the journey of the recent decades, but part of your "now" is a burden of unwanted baggage that didn't exist before. Fear, anxiety, uncertainty, self-doubt, lack of confidence. All that self-assurance used to be there, didn't it? Where did it go? Was it so connected to identity as mom, wife, daughter, employee, volunteer, boss? Now that your world has shifted forward, did all the good stuff just disappear in the move?

If you are part of a younger generation, you likely have your own set of fears and doubts. Your struggles with taking off on a road trip may fall under one of these two big umbrellas of sentiment: the demanding and relentless "I'm too busy" or the uncertain but yearning, "I am searching for something, but I don't know what." Maybe both! If your life doesn't permit much time for breathing these days, a mini road trip may be a better fit for you. For those in search of surer footing, there's plenty of encouragement to come. Your heart has led you this far into the book. Keep reading, ladies.

Doubt cares little for age. It afflicts us all. If you haven't already encountered its insidious presence, it'll show up eventually, perhaps in the form of the not-so-little voice chirping away . . . "What are you thinking? Are you crazy?" Cue the internal monsters of self-doubt, fear, and anxiety! Tell them to knock it off. You're not crazy. You're just pushing past the familiar. Maybe you're just doing the next right thing.

While I may no longer suffer from these nagging thoughts when I travel, I remember them well. And these same demons work hard to rear their heads as I write this book. "What am I thinking, writing a book at all? Am I crazy?" Fear, anxiety, and enough doubt to fill a gas tank attempt to flatten me to stillness—almost every single day.

But God. I recently read this bit of encouragement in my devotions, and I keep returning to it for assurance and confidence that I'm heading in the direction He is calling me. Written from the perspective of Jesus,

I am with you and for you. When you decide on a course of action that is in line with My will, nothing in heaven or on earth can stop you. You may encounter many obstacles as you move towards your goal, but don't be discouraged—never give up! With My help you can overcome any obstacle . . . ask Me to show you the path forward moment by moment. . . . slow down, and enjoy the journey in My Presence.

—Sarah Young, *Jesus Calling*[2]

Pray about taking off on your own. Listen to God's leading. If it's in line with His will for you, you'll know. And if it is, just do it. Follow through. Embrace your wonder, lead with your heart, create your treasure map. Seek out people and resources to guide you.

Doing so doesn't mean it won't be scary, but the God who is with you always will show you the path *moment by moment*. This is the part that speaks to me the most. He will likely not reveal to me what I need year by year or even day by day, but *moment by moment*. That means I must slow down and pay attention to where He leads—it's so easy to go off on my own and lose my way, which inevitably leads to trouble and an eventual dead end. Stay in the moment, because He will meet you, helping you to do the next right thing.

Personal Wonder

Traveling on your own will alter much of your decision-making. Solo traveling allows you to create one-of-a-kind agendas and follow through on unique impulses, to go where you feel led. You'll also see the world through a different, and likely clearer, lens.

Wonder is personal. It's unique to each of us. My own daughter, who is the person in all the world most like me, does not share the pure joy and wonder I find wandering through a bookstore. Yawn for her. Giddy pleasure for me. How is this possible? Given every opportunity to love reading, she does not. It pains me and dismays me. As close and as similar as we are, our wonder doesn't match up (although she's incredibly tolerant if there's a great coffee shop within the bookstore).

Humans have no exact match—not even identical twins are exact replicas of one another. How creative is our God! I share this as another encouragement to seek out wonder by yourself. No other person, no matter how similar, how compatible, will share your deepest passions and experience wonder in exactly the same way as you.

My daughter Sarah and I can absolutely travel together. She's probably the easiest person on planet Earth for me to travel with, precisely because we are so alike. We've enjoyed amazing adventures. We have similar expectations and don't get ruffled easily. And of course she's my kid and I love her. No doubt we'll have many an adventure together in the years to come. And yet . . .

A solo adventure is a different animal altogether. When I consider planning a trip, there is an immediate divergence between adventuring by myself versus traveling with others. From its infant stages, my motivations are completely different.

Shifting My Attention

In my world, I'm most likely going to be the planner either way, so it's not that! The shift is in my focus. When I travel with others, my attention is at least partially on my travel companions. As I plan, I am asking: at this pace, in these places and experiences, will they enjoy themselves, feel at ease, be refreshed or energized, happy with how it's all going, etc.? I'm also increasingly focused on the outward tangibles—the destinations, the lodging, the food choices, the activities—the fun. And of course, I'm thinking of the relationships among us, always hoping to nourish them. None of this is a burden—I love it!

But from the outset, my solo planning and traveling incentives are wrapped up in the wonder of looking out and not in. Of seeking the Glory of God in His creation, finding wonder in the unexpected moment, pursuing the passions of my heart. I create my treasure map with no regard to how any other person may feel and set out to learn more about the world, the God who created it all, and myself.

When you are alone, there is no one else. Brilliant, I know, but stay with me. Embarking on a trip fully of your own making, alone with your own thoughts, fears, excitement, and decisions, creates an unparalleled opportunity to discover your unique brand of wonder. A huge irony—along the way you'll find bits and pieces of you in places you've never even been. Inevitably you'll pick up some of that lost confidence and self-assurance, or whatever else it is you may have misplaced, and become more comfortable and content with YOU.

Though offering gifts of its own, the simple presence of another person, no matter how closely aligned you are, will prevent you from learning so much. You may certainly enjoy their company and it can be great fun to travel with just the right person or people. There are plenty of trips I love to take with my adult kids, friends, and family, and these trips offer their own unique gifts. But stepping out into the solo realm opens my mind. Distractions are gone. The world becomes more, well, wonder-filled!

The Hidden Upsides of Solo Travel

No matter how much planning you do (or how little!), no doubt you'll unearth many benefits of being on your own. For each advantage that falls under the category of unique-to-you and personal, there are just as many that are practical and common among us! For those of you who love a good list, this part is for you.

Solo Travel Perks

- You can take whatever you want—the whole car is yours to pack as you please!
- No one will eat your snacks.
- You don't have to share—anything.
- You get to decide when it's time for a bathroom break.
- Food for one is less expensive.
- You get to make ALL THE DECISIONS!

- There's no one to criticize your driving or your sense of direction.

- Getting "lost" becomes relative and only you decide if it matters in any given situation.

- You can do whatever you want whenever you want, which means traveling at your own pace, on your own route, eating when and whatever you like, and staying wherever you feel most comfortable.

- If you're in need of healing, there's time and space to heal.

- If you're working through fear and anxiety, you have quiet and calm, but also opportunities to stretch yourself.

- You're not responsible for the well-being of one other person on planet Earth. (Though possibly you are responsible for a pooch!)

There's more. In fact, I will argue that the most important benefits and blessings of a solo trip can't be measured quite so easily and won't be noticeable until you find yourself back in your own zip code. I love both of the following reflections, though they come from disparate sources. First, from the late Anthony Bourdain, world-renown travel writer and chef:

The journey changes you; it should change you. It leaves marks on your memory, on your consciousness, on your heart, and on your body. You take something with you. Hopefully, you leave something good behind.

It's true. Seeking wonder through traveling has left its mark on my mind, heart, and body. My perspective has shifted, and I better understand my place in the world. I am considerably more confident and mentally stronger. Most importantly, my eyes have been opened to see the grace and glory of God more clearly in my life and in the world I explore. This ability to see past the surface, to really see, has changed me.

And though Ann Voskamp wasn't writing about a road trip, she was speaking of the heart, and her eloquence provides a poignant and insightful explanation of how opening one's eyes is at the heart of change.

Always, always—first the eyes. Joy is a function of gratitude, and gratitude is a function of perspective. You only begin to change your life when you begin to change the way you see.

—Ann Voskamp, *The Greatest Gift*[3]

On Being Alone, but Connected

Going alone is not without its challenges, and there will likely be times you wish you had a pal for one thing or another. I definitely have those moments. Inevitably there are experiences I know someone else in my world would be awed by, and I wish they were there to share it with me. While I don't typically experience loneliness, I have moments of missing my family and friends, or wishing I had someone to help set up a campsite when I'm doing it for the 10th time in two weeks. On the practical side, you may wish you had someone to share the driving or the cost of lodging.

I don't have to work too hard to see the positives to each of these. In those moments when I long to connect with another human who knows me, to provide a helpful solution or just touch base on the day, it's easy to pick up the phone and call or Facetime. When something goes wrong, often our first instinct as women is to reach for someone to problem-solve with us, and sometimes we just need to talk with someone who really knows us. You can always pull out your phone and touch base for a bit before moving on. Healthy connection is important, and often fulfills that need to share and think things through.

A more introspective option is to journal or even start a personal blog for your travels. I am so grateful that I began putting my impressions on paper during that very first solo adventure. Whether you wish to write for yourself or share your adventure with others, journaling provides a safe and reflective outlet for your thoughts.

A Break from the World in Your Pocket

One caution though—for many of us, our lives are continually filled with noise, and leaving it all behind can bring a new type of anxiety. You dream of shutting off the world in your pocket—the phone, the social media, the news, the constant chatter. When the rubber literally hits the road, though, it may seem a little *too* quiet.

I encourage you to sit through this initial discomfort for a bit—discomfort will give way to something better. While I'm not suggesting you leave your phone behind altogether—you will want it for navigation and, stay with me here, to use it *as a telephone to call people* (novel!)—do consider shutting down your social media and other tempting apps. Instead, make a deliberate effort to be quiet for stretches of time while you're exploring, remembering to "be all there."

Attempting to divide our time between the entertainment *in* our car (music, podcast, phone conversations, even audio books) and the world on the other side of the windshield muddies the experience. We cannot be fully present when these pleasant distractions are drawing our mind away, no matter how much we enjoy the noise. To think freely, to day-dream, to reflect—noise cannot help but be a barrier to it all and zap your ability to experience the wonder.

I'm not advocating for completely ignoring playlists and podcasts. Music especially can offer an amazing soundtrack for your adventures! But consider providing yourself with plenty of opportunities to be quiet. You may find it lonely at the outset, but persevere. I feel confident you will discover contentment in the solitude.

As you travel solo, being totally responsible for yourself, it's inevitable that you will discover just how capable you are.

—Author unknown

Fears and Pitfalls

When you first began to consider a solo road trip, were there immediate pitfalls that came to mind? Things your insecure self quickly panicked over doing on your own? Even if the idea to seek out adventure instantly appealed, I bet you've had at least a few moments of "this is great, but I'm uncomfortable _________ by myself," or "I'm afraid to _______ by myself." Be honest!

For me, one facet of a road trip I do not like doing by myself stands out—I do not enjoy dining alone. I'd probably need a counselor to dig in deep enough to determine where this phobia comes from, but there it is. It's hardly a dealbreaker, but I'm certainly missing out on some great experiences when I give into my fear. The truth is, usually when I swallow my anxiety and go for it, the results are surprisingly wonderful!

What are your solo fears? Maybe it's showing up at a hotel by yourself or stopping at a rest area alone, shopping alone, hiking alone, doing a tour alone, camping alone. (I know, for many of you camping just isn't on the table to begin with!) It could be traveling alone—period. If that's the case, then wonderful, brave you for your willingness to at least consider taking a trip by yourself.

We all tend to avoid what we don't like (same!), and in some cases it's easy to do so. Your time on the road by yourself is a perfect opportunity to think through what's behind your solo fear and anxiety and consider how you can overcome it. If it's a restaurant issue like mine, try going into a coffee shop by yourself where there are lots of solo folks. I also find sitting outside at a restaurant is somehow easier than being in a room full of strangers. Take a book or a map or your phone. I try to wean myself from these little "crutches," but initially they are helpful. Not surprisingly, when I stop looking like I'm hiding, people are more likely to be amicable and chat. While I tend to be very friendly, as an introvert I often struggle to be the conversation starter.

Think through your solo road-tripping fears. Write them down and then consider some small first steps you might take to overcome them.

Living with Fear

I've shared in earlier chapters that my initial road trip helped me work through some significant fear and anxiety. These struggles were not connected to traveling alone. In fact, they were completely unrelated to travel and completely connected to what was a turbulent time in my life. I wrote these words in an early blog post:

Taking that first trip on my own—problem solving, reflecting, seeking wonder, looking out and not in, seeking God's glory in creation—all of these things worked quietly on my heart as the miles melted away. It wasn't a solution I had sought out, but it was how God chose to bring my fears into the light, give me time and space to wrestle with them, and then provide me with the peace to move forward without them.

Fear is crippling. It keeps us from being who God has created us to be. It takes multiple forms and targets us where we are most vulnerable—fear of failure, fear of loss, fear of judgement or of not being smart enough, pretty enough, good enough. We all relate somewhere. Most often, fear lies to us, and we believe those lies. However, there are consequences. We allow fear to steal from us, giving it unauthorized permission to rob us of peace, happiness, joy, and contentment. The result is often paralysis, as you stand frozen and seemingly unable to move in any hopeful direction.

You were not born afraid. It is learned behavior, and it likely took years for it to take root in your life. To move on from that fear takes intention, time, and space. It's likely your time alone on the road will provide you with the freedom to begin to move forward. You'll know when you're ready to call it by name and cast it aside.

When I was in my teens, I struggled with fear that kept me up at night, sometimes consuming me. It was somewhat irrational, though it came from a place that made perfect sense. After months and months of struggle, God responded to my fears. The day my much younger brother was dedicated in church, the pastor shared 2 Timothy 1:7 with us. I can't recall how in the world that connected to infant dedication, but that verse changed my heart on the spot. I keep it close always, and it's applied to countless situations in my life. Perhaps it will encourage you as you wrestle with your own fears.

> For God has not given us a spirit of fear, but of love and of power and of a strong mind.
>
> 2 Timothy 1:7

Are there specific fears that seek to take hold of you regularly? Ones that rear their heads in certain situations? Maybe there's fear in being alone. Whatever you're feeling, it may be helpful to write it down as you prepare to set out on your own.

Moving Forward

Be encouraged. You may be at a point in your life where spending time alone on a road trip is indeed not only possible but may prove to be an enormous blessing in your life. If you go, I can confidently say that heading out on your own will change you.

Traveling alone will be the scariest, most liberating, life-changing experience of your life. Try it at least once!

—Anonymous

We are standing at the corner, poised and ready to turn our attention to the practical endeavors of planning. You may carry some fear and anxiety with you for now. It's ok! The next chapters will provide time and space for you to be deliberate, to figure out what propels you forward and provides peace. You'll find your rhythm and your tempo. Before long that darling Airbnb with the fireplace will shift from daydream to reality! It will be a cheery and calming resting place for your weary and wonder-filled head. Stay the course and give yourself the grace and space to work through things at a pace that leaves you encouraged and confident.

I Wonder . . .

Take a few moments to journal (or make a list!) about what excites and intrigues you about a solo road trip.

Chapter 7

Mini Wonderings

I don't want to make mediocre art and I don't want to live a mediocre life. I recently took a walk through my neighborhood and noticed the connection between the way I walk and the way I live. I tend to walk distracted, listen to music, think through the tasks waiting for me when I get back home. I am learning how to walk like a believer, how to look ahead on the path rather than just at my feet. How to stop and touch the bark on that funny-looking tree. How to see.

—Emily P. Freeman[1]

I, too, am learning to "walk like a believer." That's truly what's at the core of this journey. Seeking wonder in the glory of God's creation has become the way I most easily and thoroughly fulfill that desire. Eyes open, head held high, looking out and not in. Emily Freeman expresses a similar longing, seeking wonder within her own neighborhood. One does not have to traverse the country to experience God's creative gifts. Mini moments of freedom and joy can be found near home. It's all in the seeing.

Perhaps brightly colored push pins, post-it notes, and pink marker populate your treasure map as you dream big dreams, your mind brimming with plots and plans. You imagine a weeks-long journey that runs like Forrest Gump across America. You want so badly to do this thing, knowing deep in your heart you're supposed to go. But the objections are mounting, and they are the real, unwavering kind. As much as you may fight it, your current circumstances are not conducive to taking an extensive adventure. At least not right now.

Relax. A big-time solo road trip may not be your next best thing. To every thing there is a season! But before you conclude that this is all just a pleasant escapist daydream, take a few minutes to sort through your conflicting thoughts and consider all the reasons it isn't working. Not because I want to change your mind, but rather so you can create a slightly different path for the here and now, knowing the grand adventure will need to wait a bit.

Create an honest list of anything that stands between you and your grand adventure. There's no judgment, no shame. Be realistic. Be honest. Call each hurdle by name. Finances? Time? Responsibilities at home or work? Maybe your hesita-

tions are more in the realm of doubt and fear. Those are no less real. Be specific and don't hold back.

Look at your list. Chances are it includes both commitments and struggles. As women we so often devote large swaths of our time to the care of others. If those responsibilities are your greatest hurdle, then give yourself permission to embrace them, even as you're increasingly eager to drive off into the sunset for a bit. Count your responsibilities as blessing, a season in your life.

If your list of obstacles is littered with internal doubts and fears, it's likely the actual road trip will be the best conqueror. Go back to the earlier chapters of encouragement and equipping for additional support! If your list of objections and concerns makes you feel a bit desperate, I encourage you to persevere—please read on! You may benefit from a road trip full of freedom and wonder more than most, though we may need to tweak it a bit.

Go through your list of challenges again. Are your named obstacles hindering you from embarking on a *lengthy* adventure, or any adventure at all? I'm betting that if you consider adjusting the amount of time you're away, you can make room in your life for a shortened journey of joy and wonder. Could you go for a day? A weekend? An afternoon? Look at the possibilities with new eyes. I believe that everyone can get away—take a break—seek wonder and bask in the presence of God's creation. Some of us just need to dream small in the beginning. Beautiful is often hidden in the small.

If you're struggling with the knowledge that this isn't your time for an extensive trip, go ahead and mourn for a bit if you need to, but don't take long. There's good news ahead! I'm a problem solver, seeker of solutions, ray of sunshine.

Just ask me. Regarding your current conundrum and list of reasons why you can't do this thing, my half-full cup is filled with thoughts to share with you. I believe if you have the desire to experience the wonder of God as you travel, He will make a way for you.

Dream Small

Give yourself permission to dream small. Earlier we discussed finding beauty in the little moments and simple things as we travel. Hang on to that no matter where you go! Here, however, we shift to seeking wonder in a small geographic footprint. God does not limit the gracious gift of His creation to wonder that can only be found hundreds of miles away.

While an extended journey provides uninterrupted days of wonder-seeking, a shorter road trip may prove to be just your size for now. It may not yet be your season to ride off into the unknown! The premise remains the same. You can still set out on your own, inspired by your passions, treasures, and tears. Seek to experience the glory of God with all of your senses—eyes wide open, ears attuned to each unique experience, smelling and tasting all that each moment has to offer.

Dreaming small simply means adventuring closer to home for a shorter period of time. With a little investigative research and imagination, I think you'll find surprising opportunities. I guarantee that no matter where you call home, both beauty and joy live nearby. Let me help get you started.

Short and Sweet
Use whatever time and resources you have to devote to a bite-sized adventure, knowing a shorter journey may be the best first step toward future lengthy road-tripping wonder. For

now, being closer to home may make it easier to be brave and to step out of your comfort zone. It likely will lead to hitting the road sooner rather than later, which is good news worth celebrating! You can still embrace your heart's cry to seek freedom, joy, and wonder through traveling on your own.

If you're unsure how to begin, employ the same approach we used to create our treasure maps. Consider starting by asking God to direct your steps, and then dive in. The difference is simply zooming in on what's nearer to you. I find this process illuminating. There are so many wonderful things to experience right under my nose, and I tend to look beyond them when I am trip planning. But when I spread out my own state map, go to the library in search of books on local places of interest, or scan for the same via the internet, I am blown away by the options. Here are two recent personal discoveries:

- In a bit of simple research about my hometown of Williamsport, Pennsylvania, I unearthed an article that revealed multiple important historical and current places of interest completely new to me! By the time I finished reading, I was already plotting a day trip in my mind. Incredible. I feel a little foolish, to be honest. Amazing bits of beauty and history I knew nothing about. No big trip needed and wonder at my doorstep.

- For most of my adult life, I have been driving the 100 miles that separate my hometown from the area where I now live. While my route back and forth deviates slightly (usually to avoid minor traffic), it has never occurred to me to follow my own road-tripping advice and get off the highways. Never, that is, until recently. It should be no great surprise that those little country roads have yielded so many moments of discovery and joy. I already realize I will need several day trips or a long weekend or two to take it all in.

Both recent discoveries opened the door to reveal bits of joy closer to home without involving significant resources or time away. I hope you find this encouraging! Dig in to your local maps, Instagram, and Facebook pages and groups. Talk to friends and family or head to the library to learn what might be right under your wheels. Plan for an afternoon or an entire day, an overnight or a full weekend. Start small and expand as you grow more comfortable and have more time.

Just Drive!

I spent some of my favorite childhood moments staring out the window of my grandmother's car. My Nan had polio as a child and never had full use of her legs. It hardly curbed her sense of adventure, though she had to dream small. She'd look at my little sister and me with a twinkle in her brown eyes, knowing the inevitable answer to her question, "Do you girls want to go for a drive on the river road?" She didn't drive much, but a friend would arrive to play chauffeur and we'd all pile in. Windows down, the promise of ice cream, and the winding river road boasting views of wide flat water, endless fields of corn, and train tracks. I can see it, smell it, taste it. Somewhere deep inside me the words "let's go for a drive" were planted in my soul, along with an ache to see around the bend.

For many of my adult years I forgot about the simple joy in "going for a drive." The concept of Sunday drives seems such a novelty of the past. I relegated the exercise to the arena of something old people did because their lives were so boring, and they had nothing else to do. I was dumb. Also, they were onto something.

Perhaps it's still a novelty, but I love it. No plan, no clue usually. Just hop in the car and pick a random back road and see where it leads. I'm rarely disappointed. If I get misplaced, I can always pull out the GPS, but it's a little bit fun to be lost for a bit. There might be a small slice of wonder in the act itself. Looking out, not in; up, not down. Anything and everything God reveals along the way is the cherry on the ice cream sundae. Always stop for ice cream!

Comfortable Wonder

Most of our destination conversations have revolved around seeking out new wonders, both the distant and close-to-home variety. We are just as able, however, to uncover joy and beauty in locations and situations already known to us. Maybe especially in those places with which we already feel a strong connection.

In his apologetic work *The Everlasting Man,* G.K. Chesterton charges us to take notice of what we know well. "Our perennial spiritual and psychological task is to look at things familiar until they become unfamiliar again." A more eloquent version of "see anew," with the added detail that the task at hand is both spiritual and psychological. How often do we walk past familiar wonder with distracted minds and bodies, missing the point entirely, or stride or shuffle past beauty with bleary-eyed distraction?

Ann Voskamp writes extensively on this topic in her wonderful book, *One Thousand Gifts: A Dare to Live Fully Right Where You Are.* She speaks repeatedly of the hard-fought joy of embracing the everyday epiphanies—the mini moments so easily overlooked. She drives home the revelatory wonder found in the simple, the common, and often the mess. While her focus isn't specifically related to travel, the heart of the message remains the same.

Your wingspan may be limited for now, but there's a gift in purposefully seeking joy and wonder in what is well worn. I am continuing to learn not to limit my philosophy regarding "wonder travel" to faraway destinations. God has granted me exceptional moments of wonder in some of the most familiar places. "The Lord my God is with me wherever I go."[2] Joy and wonder can be found wherever I am, because He is there also. Perhaps you can relate to my experiences of "wondering" close to home.

Familiar Wonder

A mere three miles from my house, a favorite getaway spot has become as known to me as my own backyard. A narrow country road mimics the gentle twists of the cold-water creek that runs alongside it. Each season these thin ribbons of road and water pair to reveal unique beauty in every direction. To be clear, however, the creek is undoubtedly the star of the show, providing unique moments of wonder from dawn to dusk.

I am not a solitary admirer of this spot, though I share early mornings with more wildlife than human life. We are all equally silent in our reverence of the early light. Except for the birds. So many chatty birds! Some folks come to stand statue-still, marveling at turkeys, wood ducks, and the occasional bald eagle. A dry fly-fishing line softly whispers through the air before settling on the water, fisherman and blue heron eyes peeled hard on the surface for a hint of interest below. There are the usual suspects—dogs and their walkers, runners and bicyclists, and the other lovers of quiet who perch at picnic tables along the water, book, and sometimes Bible, in hand.

I love the older couples in their camping chairs, feet dangling in the water, newspaper in one hand, coffee cup in the other. A good start to any day.

I have witnessed many mini moments of wonder along this clear creek. None of them newsworthy, all of them God-breathed. Three deer darting out of early morning mist to plunge into the freezing waters of winter and paddle across to the other side. A baby Baltimore oriole sitting stunned and wobbly in the middle of the road, allowing me to hold him close for a few moments before I lay him safely in the grass, his fluttering heart pulsing beneath the orange belly. I love the unending discourse of beautiful merganser ducks, their squawking a dead ringer for Charlie Brown's teacher. Wonder comes in all forms, including the three old ladies clad in their bathing suits, sitting on chairs in the middle of the creek, beers in hand, reveling in one other's company. The stories they must tell.

Familiar wonder. The canvas remains the same, but each day the Painter creates new artwork upon it. Lord, thank you for the sweet and simple opportunity to see it anew every day.

Nostalgic Wonder

I grew up in the shadow of Howard J. Lamade Stadium, mecca to all Little League baseball players and home of their World Series. For one eye-popping magical week every August, the world came to Williamsport. Growing up in small-town central Pennsylvania in the 1970s, pretty much every kid in town looked like me, talked like me, and had similar life experience (as in, practically none). To meet kids my own age from far-off places like Taiwan, Canada, Mexico, and Europe blew my little mind.

All these years later, the nostalgia factor remains high. I passed the wonder down to my own children, who enjoyed that same thrill of meeting kids from around the world and watching them play in front of 20,000+ fans. Going back now still brings joy, though Little League Week has grown into a much larger spectacle. I drink it in, taking in a few games, people-watching, running into old friends, watching new generations of 12-year-olds ooh and aah over the magic of it. I feel a great kinship with these young players, even today. I dreamed their dream—to play on the world's biggest 12-year-old stage.

It's all wonder-filled for me. Part of that stems from layers and layers of memories. I love the familiarity of it, the memories of my grandfather sitting in his aluminum lawn chair atop the hill every day watching every pitch with his schnauzer, or the voice of my Uncle Buck, broadcasting as the radio voice of Little League for most of my life. Both are gone now, but I feel their presence during that magical week (now grown to two) in August.

In all of this nostalgia, the wonder comes from deep and lasting connection.

Can you think of local places where you come into contact with wonder? Are there locations or experiences near to you that spark joy because they are familiar? Take a few moments and name them. Put into words why they are special. Consider visiting them as part of a mini-quest for wonder.

The Practice Run

Maybe you are able to embark on the big trip sometime soon, but there are a few parts of a lengthy solo journey that intimidate or concern you. These worries may be dragons you can slay with a "practice run!" Consider a short getaway to address those concerns and deal with them head-on.

If you're not sure your dog will be a great traveler, create a mini-trip close to home and find out! Maybe you have concerns about staying in an Airbnb by yourself or eating alone, or you feel a little intimidated by the driving and navigating. Whatever your potential stumbling blocks, plan a short practice adventure as a trial. If you're planning on camping alone for the first time, I strongly suggest doing an overnight at a state park or campground close to home, if only to ensure you have all the right gear!

Even if you feel pretty steady on your feet at this point, a micro-journey can be a wonderful steppingstone before you take the grand tour. It's a simplified way to work out the kinks and ease any nerves. You can address any concerns that are weighing you down, solve any issues, and ultimately build confidence and courage for the big trip!

In this immediate moment of your life, no matter how much you may want to just go for it, a smaller dream may need to fill the gap. No worries! In fact, it may be exactly the way your road-tripping adventures are meant to begin. I doubt you'll be disappointed, and God will meet you right where you are, whether you're 5 minutes or 5,000 miles from home.

Take a few moments to reflect on the benefits of embarking on a shorter road trip. What springs to mind?

Make a list of interesting local or semi-local places that you've never visited and/or experiences you've never engaged in. Choose one or two that really excite you and start planning!

Chapter 8

Personal Peace

Planning a journey into wonder is a lot like building a house. Before you can revel in the sparkly new kitchen or peacefully enjoy the porch swing, construction is required. The process may not be as enthralling and riveting as the finished product, but building a solid framework will ensure that, once complete, your home is well designed and solidly crafted so that you can relax and enjoy your life within it. Road trip preparation is much the same. If we don't devote effort to creating the practical foundation, the days on the road will be fraught with more frustration and confusion than freedom and wonder.

Just like our homes, no two adventures are exactly alike. We already know our passions, treasures, and penchants for wonder are unique to each of us. Likewise, we each have practical preferences that do not match any other's. And so we add one more element to the road trip foundation we have been building by taking a look inward to ensure awareness of our particular needs. It's not complicated or necessarily deep, nor is it selfish. It's simply ensuring we begin on solid ground.

Taking Care of You

Awareness of your day-to-day needs and the things that make each of your days manageable is an intrinsic part of creating a framework you can thrive in. To translate into "wonder-speak," if you don't take care of yourself, your pursuit of wonder will inevitably fail to inspire.

> You are the salt of the earth, but if salt has lost its taste, how shall its saltiness be restored? It is no longer good for anything except to be thrown out and trampled under people's feet.
>
> Matthew 5:13

To be at our best, we must restore ourselves daily, taking care to be fed both practically and spiritually. I'd like to add another component to this self-care framework. I call them my "bits of wonder." Those little moments of light, of wishfulness, of possible imaginations. They're bite-sized moments that you can tap into on any given day. All are essential framework for the larger wonder puzzle.

Bits of Wonder

These mini moments won't correlate to pins on your treasure map, yet they're no less important to your daily well-being and your pursuit of wonder than your sought-after destinations and moments of grand adventure. Planning a solo road trip typically begins with visions of mountaintop experiences as you joyride into the unexplored places, but I'll bet that at least a smidge of your compulsion to take a trip on your own stems from a desire to enjoy a few pint-sized treats and comforts as well. I'm referring to those little moments of indulgence that cannot coexist in your current reality of norm and noise.

What bits of wonder do you dream about? Sipping coffee as you watch the sun rise, choosing your own music in the car without sighs of disapproval from passengers, enjoying uninterrupted quiet time? Perhaps nothing quite so tangible, but your yearning drifts toward feelings of peace, freedom, simple joy. The pull of these mini moments can be just as compelling as a bucket-list destination, and for good reason.

Right now, your days seem too busy, your life too stretched to do anything other than momentarily imagine time and space for these. But on the road? Deep breaths and yes, please! There can be both room and time for the little things that speak to your unique sense of peace and joy. Whether the day on the road has been easy or chock full of obstacles, gloriously wonder-filled or just a little "blah," it's vital to create time and space for these little wonder moments.

There's something *self*-satisfying here, but also *soul*-satisfying. In Matthew 5:13, Jesus recognizes that His followers will grow weary, and that we are good for nothing if we are not restored. That need for restoration is part of what compels us to step out and seek wonder, to renew and transform our minds, to rest and rejuvenate. When you devote time for yourself and your relationship with Christ—when you take a few moments just to be—you replenish your emotional and spiritual tank. What not-so-magically results is peace.

Take a few moments to name your "bits of wonder." Remember to dream small here! Maybe it's watching a sunrise? Finding a hidden stream or waterfall? Sitting quietly in a cute coffee shop? Wandering through a bookstore? As you plan your days on the road, make a point to incorporate a few into each day.

Peace of Mind for Your Heart and Head

Putting names to your basic needs and ensuring they are incorporated into your days on the road are essential. I could also refer to this little section as "daily stuff that makes you happy" or "a daily attempt to kick stress to the curb."

Let's face it. There are things that each of us build into our day for peace of mind. There are also things we do because if we don't, we know it's gonna be a struggle. There's no shame in it. When we travel, we tend to alter our habits a bit and ignore some of our usual routines. It's part of what we look forward to when we leave home! Sifting through what counts as "need," however, is a worthwhile exercise. In fact, it's vitally important that you know what these little items of requirement are before you even begin to dig into the details of your adventure. Disregarded, they'll lie in wait and rear their ugly non-caffeinated heads at you, attempting to ruin an otherwise perfectly wonderful day.

I won't call them non-negotiable, because it's important to leave room for flexibility, but to identify these elements as things you "strongly desire" seems appropriate. Ultimately there are two separate categories to consider—the practical things and then what I'll call the heart-check list. To prime the pump of your own thinking, I'll share a few of my strongly desired basics and a little anecdote about what can happen when I neglect them. Whether I'm waking up in a tent in Wisconsin or an Airbnb in Maine, these elementals help me get my head, heart, and body ready for the day.

The Head Stuff

I've traveled enough to know there are a few uber-practical things that will give me a much better chance at fully enjoying and engaging in the day. In any 24-hour period, I covet:

a. A shower (or at the very least clean clothes!)

b. Caffeine

c. A long walk or hike

d. At least one healthy-ish meal that I eat sitting somewhere other than behind the wheel of my SUV

e. A touchpoint with family

f. An engaging route

g. Arrival at my daily destination before sunset

I'll drill down a bit on some of these. Over time, I've learned (thanks, Covid) that I really will survive if I don't shower every day. However, I will not fare as well if there isn't some sort of caffeine coursing through my veins by late morning. Some of you are nodding your heads in vehement agreement with this. If not, don't judge. We all have our vices, and I currently enjoy mine a little too much to give it up!

Though my kids are in their 20s, I try to touch base quickly with them each day or let them know when I'm going to be off the grid. I'm also a daughter, and I know I can provide a little peace for my parents if I check in periodically with them.

I am happier when I drive a road that I can engage with and enjoy, and it is always my desire to arrive at my destination for the night before dark. I don't want to miss anything, and if I'm camping, I don't ever want to be that person who's trying to put up a tent in the dark. No way. I want to be the girl who's completely set up with dinner in front of the fire as the sun goes down.

I don't need it all every day—that's a little unreasonable and being flexible is important. Rigidity sucks all the fun out of the adventure. But keeping these needs in mind while I'm pre-trip planning and as I begin each day on the road helps me begin (and proceed!) in peace.

The Heart Stuff

The other half of our self-care framework is more spiritual in nature and lays the groundwork for experiencing gratitude and wonder. When I'm on the road, I'm extra cognizant of the world around me. I am in search of the unexpected, of beauty, of peace, and joy in the experience. For the best opportunity to find these each day, I'm infinitely better off if I begin slowly and with purpose. Incorporating the following intentional moments in my morning helps me focus.

A checklist for heart health seems counter-intuitive, so what follows provides a little more detail than your average inventory. Perhaps unremarkable, these few things ensure I am prepared to take on the day. For me, it really boils down to time spent with Jesus.

- **Prayer**—Making plenty of time to pray tops my list, and I am more likely to do this while walking in the early morning. I feel closer to God when I am reveling in His creation, so praising him for the beauty of His world is often where I begin.

- **A Spirit of Thankfulness and Anticipation**—While not unique to road-tripping, being purposeful in these areas inevitably sets my priorities in order, no matter what the day may bring! Investing time to orient my spirit toward thankfulness and anticipation for the opportunity to go beyond wandering sets my compass toward the Giver of all good things and makes space to step into wonder.

- **Devotional Reading of Scripture**—God promises that His Word does not go out without accomplishing its purpose. While I'm not always successful, every day that I carve out those minutes to read His Word comes back to bless my day abundantly. I also love listening to scripture on my phone while I'm driving or just getting ready in the morning.

This focused time reminds me to look out and not in, to keep my eyes wide open. I want to see and experience wonder, to meet my Maker in the world He designed me for, and designed for me. Keeping my heart and eyes fixed on Him helps ensure that I won't miss what He has prepared for the day ahead. Even when I bring my burdens to the day, as I make my requests known to God, He will guard my heart and my thoughts. Walking with Him through all of it, acknowledging Him and His love for me and for His creation, I find peace and joy in the journey of each day.[1]

> This is the day the Lord hath made; we will rejoice and be glad in it!
>
> Psalm 118:24

Wonder in Spite of Myself

I have discovered that I can wonder when I'm dirty and haven't had enough sleep or a decent cup of tea, but it's not really pretty and I can easily make a mess of things. This unfortunately leads to a bad attitude that allows the day to go sideways. More than a few lessons have been learned along the way, and I try to do better each time!

The following adventure took place in northwestern Montana. Lexi the Golden and I were endeavoring to reach Glacier National Park prior to its official 6:00 a.m. opening one July morning. The number of daily entry passes was limited, and I had been unable to procure a coveted ticket. Word on the street was that if you showed up prior to 6:00, you could enter through the unmanned booth without one, and that was my only shot at entrance. Additionally, a wide swath of forest fires in the north threatened to impede the views of this sought after destination, and the smell of burning pine drifted into my dreams.

From
"On the Road with Stress and Anxiety"

The day did not begin enthusiastically as I took down my tent beside the very chilly Flathead Lake at 4:00 a.m. in pitch black, trying not to disturb fellow campers. A mix-up at the campground meant we did not have a spot to return to for the night, so at the last minute I had chosen to go to Glacier a day early, with no certainty of claiming a campsite either back in Flathead or within the national park. We had to pack up and take everything with us, hopeful that upon our return there would be a place to lay our very weary heads if we couldn't find a spot within Glacier. I left in my pajamas, though I think I may have brushed my teeth. Maybe. Also, no caffeine. Again, NO caffeine.

I, quite literally, wasn't a happy camper. Could this possibly be worth it?

As we drove, I stressed about not making it before 6:00 a.m. I also stressed that the 6:00 a.m. thing wasn't a thing. Then what? Ugh. I needed a shower, and real clothes for starters. And gas. Was there time to stop to fill the tank? Maybe it could wait? More stress. And what about all these smoky skies? Surely Glacier would be cloudy at best. And finally, where the heck were we going to stay?

And so it was that I headed northwest on the hour drive to the park, ridiculously ridden with anxiety as the skies lightened around me, seeing nothing but the gas gauge and the time on the clock. This is the textbook example of the opposite of what I am all about. I was in Montana on an amazing road trip!!! I needed to get it together.

Big breaths, slow prayers for God to open my eyes and heart to all He wanted me to see and experience that day. Radio now on with inspiring music. I sailed through the gate at 5:37 (yes!) with plenty of gas in the tank, and we were in! My heart slowed, and within minutes all the unreasonable anxiety of the morning was lifted with the dawn as a gorgeous azure blue sky reined over us.

I look back and see a foolish girl who knew better than to get all caught up in her self-made drama. I also recognize the importance of paying heed to some of my very basic needs.

Perhaps it was starting the day in the ink cold black of 4:00 a.m. That wasn't my best set-up for a day of wonder and experiencing the glory of God. I thought I had planned well enough to pull off stealing away into the morning darkness without any stress or anxiety, but I had taken my fundamental needs for granted.

Lessons were learned. Ensuring time and space for at least a little bit of what gives me a sense of peace first thing in the morning is important. If a day ends up going sideways, I handle it all much better if I've taken care of the essentials at the outset. It's a little like the philosophy of making your bed first thing every morning. No matter how unpredictable the rest of the day's events prove, you've begun, not only with something positive but a tangible victory, however small. In terms of this particular early, messy morning, even giving myself the opportunity to change my clothes and leave 10 minutes earlier (time for gas and caffeine) would have changed the tone from the start.

The other takeaway (no surprise!) was God redeemed it all and used it for good. The incredible wonder of His world quickly and rightfully overshadowed my mini-meltdown and settled me back into pajama-clad peace. Though I wasn't at my faithful best earlier in the day, our God ensured that my morning mess was no match for the majesty of His creation. In hindsight it was an epic day made more so by the muddled beginning. My time in Glacier remains one of the most captivating and memorable days in my road-tripping history, though I still rue the lack of caffeine and my choice to wear pajamas!

Moving Ahead

Devoting time to think through your own needs in advance of your travels will provide you with some peace of mind each day and will help lay the foundation for a wonderful adventure. Things will go wrong, plans will go sideways, but you will be better able to take on the unknown challenges of the day!

Your Head and Heart Lists

Just as every other facet of preparing and experiencing wonder is individual to you, your daily needs are unique as well. The specifics are endless. If you're more extroverted, you may need to spend time in the presence of plenty of people some days. Perhaps your strong preference is a decent hotel each night. Maybe you need Oreos or Starbucks (no judgement here) or your favorite true-crime podcast.

Perhaps your spiritual "to dos" include time for worship, journaling, or even listening to music. It may be as simple as a verse for the day, or a quiet moment of thanksgiving. You may find that a peaceful walk puts you in the proper mindset for the day ahead. Consider what really may be non-negotiable, or at least high priority. As you plan your days, keep this top of mind.

I Wonder . . .

Take some time to think about and write down what your daily necessities might be.

Part Two

Pivoting Toward the Practical

C.S. Lewis didn't have a road trip in mind when he penned these words. During this World War II era sermon, he spoke to a British nation in the midst of immense chaos and loss. How palpable the heart tug to "experience" and "be united with beauty" must have been during such a frightening time. Surely those who heard this man preach hung on his every word.

Now 80 years later, those same words resonate deeply as I seek wonder in the creation of this same God of the universe. This utter compulsion to ferret out beauty I can "bathe in" and "become part of" moves me each morning.

I share C.S. Lewis's words for a reminder as we forge ahead into the practicalities of how to design our days on the road. We will think through how far to travel on any given day, where to eat and sleep, what to pack, how to budget and navigate. If you're a planner, you have been waiting for these chapters!

BUT (caps intended!), let us never lose sight of the goal of wonder: to seek out the glory of God in the world He has created for us. It's so easy for me to become obsessed with the details and miss the point entirely. I hope to equip you to find the balance between an appropriate amount of preparation and an insatiable joy as you seek wonder on the road.

Chapter 9

Big Picture Planning

Every day we travel, we enjoy the privilege of seeking wonder in the world God breathed into existence. During the first five days of the creation, God consistently called all that He had created "good." On the sixth day, God made man in His image, and gave him dominion over it all, telling Adam and Eve that He had made everything for their use and entrusting it to their care.

God wants us to *see* what He has made. He longs for us to enjoy it, treasure it, revel in it, experience Him within it. We are called to go out with our eyes open. To "find all (He) has prepared for you in this precious day of life." Wonder isn't just passing by, but really *seeing*.

As we dive more and more into the practicalities and inevitable checklists that come with preparing for your adventure, hold on to the anticipation of exploring and seeking God-designed wonder. No amount of planning should overshadow your pursuit of awe and joy.

On the surface it may appear there's a conflict between pragmatic preparation and the creative joy of heading off into the unknown, windows down, hair flying. However, I don't believe they work in opposition, but, rather, that they create a harmonious relationship.

Personal Planning Profile

In the previous pages, you created head and heart lists of daily needs. These serve as the first pieces in designing a solid foundation for your adventure. The next chapters will guide you through the work of creating a plan that checks all the practical boxes and fits your specific personality while allowing plenty of room for wonder. You'll have ample opportunity to think through each area and consider what works best for you. The result? A strategy that builds confidence and anticipation for your solo adventures—a one-of-a-kind Personal Planning Profile.

What's Your Travel Style?

Devising a wonder-filled, low-stress road trip requires a dose of self-awareness. Understanding your planning personality is the best place to begin and will make the path to designing your trip much smoother.

Your planning personality refers to your style of planning. While you are unlikely to fit neatly into any one category, you'll likely resonate more with either the intense and deliberate planner who leaves nothing to chance or the flying-more-by-the-seat-of-your-SUV girl. There's no right or wrong way to do it, but thinking through your unique travel style in advance allows you to plan in a way that makes you comfortable.

Consider each of these extreme planning profiles—do you see a bit of yourself in one or both?

The Power Planner

Known for creating a checklist for her checklists, the Power Planner wakes up most mornings, pencil in hand, prepared to declare war on her many to-do lists. Few moments are left unscheduled. Prior to heading out on a road trip, she creates a 3-inch binder that includes inventory for every item in her vehicle and a pages-long spreadsheet to budget each category and subcategory of spending. During her travels, she tracks her spending to the penny. Her printed out and highlighted maps include daily and hourly targets, as well as a designation for every choice of road, rest area, and restaurant. In order to check the wonder box each day, she has a list with all the intended "aha moments" calculated, along with time permitted for joy and tears in each instance, and a color-coded graph measuring planned excitement and joy against the reality.

The Random Rambler

Waking up on a random Tuesday, the Random Rambler thinks, "Today . . . today is a good day for a road trip." And off she goes. Where? No one, including herself, has a clue. How long, how far? Debatable. What she'll eat and where she'll stay? Determined as each need arises, but certainly not before. Everything about her travel is spontaneous, with little forethought to money or destination. She'll come back when she's done. She is certain that wonder is found only in the impromptu and impulsive, in figuring it out as she goes and hoping she doesn't run out of gas in the middle of nowhere. But if she does, no worries! It's part of the story and she's up for it.

Finding a Balance

Does merely reading either of these descriptions stress you out? Regardless of the answer, I'm willing to wager you see a bit of yourself in each, though chances are you are neither a full-blown power planner nor a 100% free-spirited rambler. Rarely are we quite so black and white! I share these over-blown caricatures to provide you with an opportunity to consider each extreme as a planning style, and perhaps laugh at yourself a little bit if needed!

I resonate with aspects of both these travelers, though I fall more on the side of the planner. That should come as no surprise, since I am writing this book! Too much planning, however, creates self-inflicted stress and gets in the way of my goal of wonder. I never want to feel like I'm on a hard and fast schedule when I'm on a road trip, but I do find peace in having arranged certain specifics. Alternatively, if I was winging it entirely, I'm not sure I would feel free for long. For me freedom doesn't equate to zero structure. Freedom and wonder are found when the balance is right, and I know myself well enough to create a structure that works for me.

Undergirding that balance between spontaneity and meticulous planning is one other vital element. My entire planning process is supported by prayer. Earlier I shared with you my morning prayer as I begin each day on the road, but what about everything leading up to the journey itself? I've learned it's vital to invite God into my decision-making and allow Him to lead me where He wants me to go. I know I will not make great choices if I rely solely on my own mind. Trust in the Lord with all your heart. In all your ways acknowledge Him, and He will make straight your paths.[1] Ask Him to direct your paths from the outset!

Taking time in advance to consider the style of planning you're most comfortable with will allow space for you to relax and feel freedom in your choices when you're on the road. I'll add here that if you're unsure of your planning style, then consider how you manage life at home. Knowing what fits your lifestyle in your daily environment could very well be a clue to what would make you comfortable in your initial road-tripping adventure.

There are caveats, of course. For example, if you know that you're an obsessive checklist planner, you may recognize that part of your decision to hit the road relates to a desire to let go of your firm grip on controlling every aspect of your day. For others, making the decision to give this a try is enough of a deviation from life at home, so being a little more set in your planning may provide a level of confidence and comfort you need. It really is a personal choice.

Spend a few moments considering what style of planning would give you the most confidence. What are the areas, if any, where you likely will desire some control? In what areas do you think you are more prone to "wing it"?

The Pillars of Planning

Once you determine your style, then you're ready for big picture planning. Whether you are setting out to wonder for a month or just a day or two, taking some time to realistically anticipate a general strategy you love is worth its weight in free gasoline. (That's like gold these days, right?)

This isn't about plotting and planning the details of each day in advance. What I'm referring to here is laying out the broader scope of a plan you are comfortable with. One that provides confidence and the right amount of flexibility. It's partly about sitting back and reflecting on what will bring you joy, how to travel comfortably and allow room for expectancy and wonder each day. Even if you plan to wing it a good bit of the time, considering a plan for the big picture will help you make the most of your spontaneity!

Your "heart and head" lists from the previous chapter factor in here. They serve as the first part of the framework. But how do we take the leap from making sure you get a good cup of coffee and a shower all the way to a full-blown plan? What are the essentials to complete the building project? After years of trial and error (and plenty of wandering and wondering!), I believe these six pillars of planning will allow you to create a travel profile that sets you up for wonder.

- Budget
- Time
- Distance
- Navigation
- Lodging
- Food

Regardless of how and where you will road trip, all six will factor into your adventures, and it's essential to understand the big picture of how they play into your decision-making. As we investigate each, keep in mind that they constantly overlap and intertwine. For example, we cannot discuss creating a budget for a trip without considering food or lodging, nor can you plan the distance of your travel without heeding the time it will take you to make the trip.

Each is vital enough to warrant its very own lengthier discussion, and the next chapters are devoted to drilling down into the details. For now, let's create a working knowledge of how each fits into the bigger picture.

Framing It Out

My own general approach to planning a road trip is pretty intuitive after all these years, though I've given each of these six essentials tons of thought and continue to tweak them accordingly as I learn more about my own needs and style. While every day on the road plays out in its own unique manner, I am confident knowing I have created a plan that works for me. Not only does my foundational knowledge aid in my advance planning, but it helps me get back on track when the unexpected happens.

Sharing an example of how I approach each of these pillars will help you think about your own preferences, which will be unique to you! Remember that for this chapter, I am providing insight into the big picture of planning. The specifics of every trip will be different, but my consistent larger-scale planning remains similar for each adventure. As you read, I encourage you not to become overwhelmed by the length of the trip I use as an example! Whether your trip is 22 days or 2 days, the principles for creating a travel plan remain the same!

How It Works

Last summer, I embarked on a three-week road trip. Along with my faithful companion golden retriever, Lexi, I traveled from Central Pennsylvania to Wyoming and Colorado before heading back east. Here is a brief overview of my strategy.

Budget

This is where my planning begins, and I always have a budget.

Generally, I have a set sum to spend on a trip. I determine that number far in advance and usually save for it. My greatest expenditures are gas and lodging, followed by food. I do my best to scope out in advance what I think I'll need to spend on gas, and then determine from there how I should manage my lodging and food and other smaller expenses.

Time

- I set a start date and an end date (within a day or two) for every trip.

- I determine my main destination(s) and estimate how long I plan to stay there.

- I consider how long I want to spend exploring en route, dividing up travel days and wandering spots.

On this particular trip I had two destinations: Sheridan, Wyoming, and a small town in southern Colorado. Here's how I decided to break up my travels.

1. PA > Sheridan = 7 days

2. Remain in Sheridan—5 days

3. Sheridan > Colorado = 7 days

4. Remain in Colorado—4 days

5. Colorado > home—as fast as possible!

Time, as a planning pillar, has a second component, and that is knowing what works best for me as I begin and end each day on the road.

1. Between 9:00 and 10:00 a.m.—get on the road for the day

2. Between 5:00 and 7:00 p.m.—arrive at destination for the night

Distance

I do not spend time worrying about total distance traveled. My concern is typically how to break the trip up into reasonable daily chunks. On a long trip like this one, my general goal is to spend fewer than 6 hours driving each day.

1. On this journey, I needed to cover 2,500 miles in the first week, so most days I expected to drive at least 6 hours. I did, however, build fun mini-destinations into each day to give both Lexi and myself a break and provide something to look forward to. I managed to keep the driving to approximately 5-6 hours a day.

2. On the week's drive from Wyoming to Colorado, I purposely wandered to new places and drove about 1,500 miles, though the direct route would have been a mere 600 miles. Each day I spent an average of 3.5 hours in the car.

Time and distance work together in the planning process for me. I mapped out how this was all going to work before I left home, so I was comfortable with the plan as it unfolded, and it left plenty of room for spontaneity.

Navigation

Navigation is the most adaptable part of the process for me. I spend time in advance looking at the options for getting from A to B on any given day, but many decisions are made en route. I cannot imagine a trip without flexibility! Sometimes I finalize a plan for a particular day in advance; other times my approach is more fluid.

1. For the first leg of this trip, I planned:

    a. My basic route to Wyoming over those first seven days

    b. My reservations for each night

2. During the second week, I knew a few places I wanted to visit and explore, but as I had an entire week to cover much less ground, I intentionally built in plenty of time for wandering each day. Still, I had a general idea of how I'd navigate it all and a few reservations to anchor down the trip.

3. Leaving Colorado, my goal was just to come straight home, so that was easy. Find the nearest superhighway and drive like mad.

Lodging

In my case, lodging significantly drives my overall plan as well as my budget. I prefer to know in advance where I'll be spending the night, though it doesn't always happen that way.

On this particular trip, I had a plan for each of the days leading from Pennsylvania to Wyoming.

- 3 campgrounds

- 2 hotels

- 1 Airbnb

For the following week, I secured reservations at three different campgrounds, but that was it. I didn't completely wing it, because I had researched enough to know there were plenty of options available in the areas where I planned to end each day. This can be tricky, though, and I've learned when I'll be comfortable figuring things out at the last minute versus when I'll prefer to have things nailed down.

Food

I do a significant amount of planning regarding food.

As it pertains to each day, I pack tons of snacks, pre-make certain foods for easy meals that don't have to be heated up, and do not eat out very much, especially on the front end of the trip. It becomes harder later in the trip, when all my initial goodies are gone! Typically, I have what I need in my car for breakfast, lunch, and for snacking, and then my dinner comes from my cooler or the occasional restaurant or grocery store stop.

Managing Expectations

Homing in on your travel style and figuring out how you will approach each of these six essential planning pillars goes a long way toward equipping you for a great adventure. These blend together to create a personal profile you can bank on as you plan, both in advance of your journey and in response to events during it.

Regardless the length or distance of the trip, investing time to consider each of these pillars will save you plenty of confusion and stress when you are on the road. How you choose to handle each of these is perfectly wonderful and unique to you. You won't get it all right the first time, but building a foundation in advance and clarifying your approach will allow you to manage those moments when things fall apart.

Before you read one more sentence, know this: You're

going to make a mess of it some days. It's okay! Chances are those days will make for plenty of unexpected memories and learning moments. But feeling lost *every* day (not literally, but maybe) without any real sense of how to move forward will rob you of your confidence, your peace, and your joy. It will get frustrating very quickly. Having one day that's a mess is fine. You get up the next day with a clear head toward your next step and you jump back on track. It's when you've failed to pay attention in advance to what works for you—that's when it goes sideways.

Winging It—A Cautionary Tale

Several summers ago, I embarked on my most expansive road trip to date. One month, 20 states, and over 8,000 miles. After several years of road-tripping, my framework was pretty trusty, and I was a confident explorer and wonderer. About halfway through this big adventure, I arrived in the Seattle area with the primary goal of visiting the San Juan Islands, which sit just off the coast of Washington's northwest corner. This stop was an intended part of my ten-day wanderings from Washington to Colorado. For those ten days, I had no specific plan and had intentionally decided to experiment with full-scale fly-by-the-seat-of-my-pantsness to see how I managed.

Definition for "fly by the seat of your pants": to do something difficult without the necessary skill or experience.

—Cambridge Dictionary

Note the "without the necessary skill" part. Even though I had plenty of road-trip experience, I lacked the necessary skill for diving into the full-blown unknown.

The first of those ten days remains one of my least favorite of all my road-tripping days—ever. Don't misunderstand—I'm all for spontaneity. More often than not, that's when I come face-to-face with wonder. But that day, I ignored everything I knew about myself as a traveler and traded in common sense for reckless spontaneity. I learned in one incredibly long and overwhelming day that trying something new doesn't work for me if it's completely haphazard. I personally need some parameters.

I know that may sound lame to the true rambler. But ditching everything that works for me ultimately left me stressed, indecisive, and with no room for wonder. I tried to embrace the high adventure of the day, but I failed. Why? In part because it rarely goes well when a notoriously slow processor (that's me) makes multiple quick decisions, which are most often followed up by additional poor decisions. My goal each day is to meet my God as I wonder in His Creation, but instead I ended up focused on my frustration. I missed all the joy. I wasn't able to stay in the moment, keep my eyes open, and see what He had for me that day.

The morning began in the city of Everett, Washington, which sits alongside Interstate 5 just north of Seattle, a mere 93 miles northwest of Bremerton, Washington, my eventual destination that day. Driving the roads around the southern end of Seattle to get there, the trip takes an hour and 40 minutes. If you choose the scenic route, across the Puget Sound by ferry, add half an hour to the journey. For me, on a day full of mishaps, confusion, and general bad decision-making, the trip took ten and a half hours and spanned 313 miles.

I'm rarely in favor of the get-there-as-directly-as-possible highway approach. And had this day gone well, I'm sure I would have found a happy medium between the direct highway route and my eventual reality. The ridiculous mess I made of this day was not caused by an inability to read a map or follow a GPS. Nope. I began with no plan and crammed what should have been three days' worth of adventuring into one very long, frustrating July day. Let's add a large dose of poor judgement on my part on at least three or four occasions.

And so I set off with two seemingly brilliant ideas. First, to head north (yes, north!) to a small town near the Canadian border that had been highly recommended to me by a shopkeeper a few days earlier. Second, as I drove north full of anticipation for adventure, I decided on a whim to check in with a high school friend who had moved to the area several years before. Was she around? Available? She was! Amazing! She lived in Bremerton and we could have dinner together. Both ideas seemed wonderful, and I had a plan, which gave me peace.

But I failed to consider time and distance in a place I'd never been, or how to traverse a giant city where water travel is a part of daily navigation. I didn't consider rush hour traffic, nor did I appreciate the massive size of the greater Seattle area.

I'm writing this years later, and my head is currently pounding recounting that day. Why? Yes, it was long, but nothing truly bad happened. In fact, I enjoyed a lovely morning strolling around the quaint town of Lynden and ended the evening relaxing at a waterfront restaurant in Bremerton with a high school friend I'd only seen once since 1984. Even still, it reigns as one of my least favorite days of travel ever.

I had failed to honor what I know about myself and what works for me.

- I rushed out on a whim early that morning without taking care of my daily routine.

- I started with no plan, then with little thought, committed to being in two places that were in completely opposite directions.

- I had no appreciation or understanding of the ferry system.

- I ignored my initial intention for being there—to spend time exploring the islands.

- I didn't pay attention to what I know helps me seek wonder. Time to explore, slow pace, etc.

A few additional takeaways from the day. Though it's clear I attempted to handle that day in my own strength, God was there with me, protecting me and saving me from myself and my foolish ways. He also graced me with two amazing moments of wonder I reveled in from the driver's seat.

At one point, evening rush-hour traffic forced me into a slow crawl southbound on Interstate 5. I continued to grumble (both my heart and my stomach) about all the hours yet to drive, but when I glanced into the rearview, the glorious Mount Baker filled every inch of the mirror. Part of the irony was that earlier in the day, when I was a mere 30 miles from the mountain, I had unsuccessfully scrambled around trying to find the best vantage point to admire this massive snow-capped peak. Now, a full 100 miles from the summit (and many hours, ferry rides, and bad decisions later), my rearview mirror provided the perfectly framed picture.

Another thirty minutes and just a few miles further down the highway, I almost rear-ended the car in front of me as I came around a bend. Mouth agape, I drank in the staggering beauty of Mount Rainier spread out before me. Though it was easily 100 miles to the south, it filled my windshield and appeared close enough to touch. I know now that, on most days, both of these mountains remain hidden behind rain, clouds, and dense fog. But on this magnificent sunny day, God made sure I could see them both—one before me and one behind. Wonder prevailed.

My ten-day "seat of my pants" experiment had gotten off to a rocky start, though blessings emerged that day. The frustration weighed heavy, but I gained confidence in handling new situations. I knew if I managed every day on the road like that one, I'd be miserable in a hurry, not to mention stressed out.

The next morning, I awoke to views of the distant Olympic mountains over the bay near Bremerton. Deep breath; joy in the morning. I was able to recalibrate and revert to what I know works for me—a long walk to begin, time to talk with the God who would lead me through the day, and some good suggestions from the locals on navigating time and distance for the near future. I would once again wander into new territory, but I better understood when a plan was needed and when to fly by my seat. It was a little thrilling, after all!

I Wonder . . .

Before we explore each of the six planning pillars in depth, take a few moments to write down any thoughts or concerns about how you anticipate approaching each. Which ones seem easier to manage? Which ones make you nervous?

- Budget
- Time
- Distance
- Navigation
- Lodging
- Food

Chapter 10

It's Time

It's a terrible thing, I think, in life to wait until you're ready. I have this feeling now that actually no one is ever ready to do anything. There is almost no such thing as ready. There is only now. And you may as well do it now. Generally speaking, now is as good a time as any.

—Hugh Laurie

Investing your time and treasure to read this guide speaks to your sense of curiosity and desire for wonder, if not your readiness. Planning your first adventure may still feel daunting, though you hopefully feel inspired to make it happen! You have no doubt trudged through valleys and skipped along the mountaintops in your world, yet the all-by-your-self-adventure is a new mission. And you are plotting with purpose—to seek wonder as you meet God in the midst of His creation. Trust Him in all things, including the planning of your adventure. Acknowledge Him in every step you take. He will make your paths straight.

Are you ready? Perhaps as Hugh Laurie blithely puts it, "Generally speaking, now is as good a time as any." At this juncture in our tale, it's time. Time to discern just where on your treasure map your first adventure will take you. Time to create a plan and schedule that translates to freedom and wonder on the road. Time to examine the essential pieces of planning and design them to meet your unique needs and expectations. And yes, time to pull out the checklists and worksheets!

Big Picture Connections

As we enter into this next phase of planning, you may confidently know where your adventure will lead. If you haven't chosen your destination or path just yet, you can still move forward and think through many of the specifics. Once you cement those decisions, the road will be paved for more concrete conclusions.

As we approach each of the essential pieces, I could provide suggestions, possibilities, pitfalls, and cumbersome step-by-step instructions that would ultimately undermine your need to figure it out and create your own path to wonder. We've come too far for me to hijack the process now! Designing your adventure plan requires making decisions about each of the essential pieces. This is all you! You get to make every single choice. As you begin plotting out your grand adventure, my role here becomes much like the proud parent—to provide guidance in each area, offer suggestions and support to help avoid some of the stumbling that happens both in the planning and the execution, and to cheer you on.

Let's begin with a few broad thoughts relating to the six-pillars planning. Here's the list again for easy reference:

- Budget
- Time
- Distance
- Navigation
- Lodging
- Food

1. **Think through all six!** Ignoring any of these pillars will add many a bump in the road. It's worth your time and effort to consider in advance how you'll deal with each. As the sole decision-maker, you alone determine your planning style, because you are the only one who can be trusted to know what will work for you.

2. **Recognize that they intertwine.** It's impossible to systematically check off your planning of each pillar, one at a time. This will hold true while you're on the road as well. The causes and effects are constant, and you'll soon discover that it's necessary to consider them simultaneously as they overlap.

3. **Consider your "sweet spots."** Set expectations for yourself that fit your comfort zone. While taking a solo road trip provides plenty of opportunity to be spontaneous and try new things, there's wisdom in sticking with some of the basics that make you, well, you!

   For instance, if you know you're best in the early mornings and fade out by late afternoon, plan your days with this key piece of understanding in mind.

Maybe you have trouble sitting still for more than a few hours at a time. If so, it's probably not wise to plan too many days with massive amounts of driving. If you struggle with back issues, now is probably not the time to ignore your need to sleep on a good mattress most nights. While a solo road trip provides wonderful opportunities to see anew, be careful not to create an environment that ignores your known areas of comfort and happiness!

4. **Take planning breaks.** Figuring out the when and how and where of your adventure can be so exciting! But likely you'll hit a wall at some point. I always do. Give yourself permission to step back and walk away for a while. Take as long as you need to put your adventure puzzle together. For some, this process can be a bit torturous. If you know that about yourself, you may be better served with a little more fly-by-the-seat-of-your-pantsness on some days.

When I get overwhelmed with mapping out a portion of a trip, whether it's where I'm stopping, the route I may take, or where I'll stay the night, I entertain a few possible strategies. See if any of these resonate with your planning personality.

- I come back later with fresh eyes and doggedly dig back in until I figure it out.

- I throw in the towel and decide to wing it that day.

- I consider that I may need to scrap that part of my plan and start over. If I'm truly trying to put a square peg in a round role, it's just not going to fit.

None of these are rocket science, and in the end, I tend to go with my gut. It usually turns out great!

A Note About Resources

While all six Pillars of Planning consistently overlap and affect one other, each deserves individual attention. One caveat—I have lumped "time" and "distance" together as you cannot consider one without the other. Take your time with each of the chapters to come. You may already feel confident in some areas, where others will be full of new thoughts and information.

In each chapter, you'll find discussions and encouragements, specific tips, and suggestions to aid you in your planning. To help take both guesswork and busywork out of the process, you'll find consumable resources to download and print at www.wonderbingtravel.com/book-resources. I've created templates and checklists for each essential area, as well as plenty of website links. Let's get started!

Chapter 11

Begin With a Budget

A budget isn't about restricting what you can spend. ***It permits you to spend without guilt or regret.*** *Once again, know that budgeting habits increase your freedom, power, and ease in life.*

—Dave Ramsey

Once I settle on my main destination for any given journey, I consider my budget. I firmly believe that budgeting for each of my trips is as important as any other decision I make regarding travel. I realize that, for many people, the mere mention of the word "budget" makes them want to hide under the covers, or at least put fingers in their ears and scream until it goes away. Please don't. It's not a bad word. It's a blessing.

Having a budget for any venture is freeing. Having a budget for travel, if thought through properly, contributes to a trip that can be both guilt and care free. Knowing where your money is going builds confidence, and we all want to feel unflappable and self-assured in our travels!

I am neither a budget nor a money expert. During my quarter century of marriage, I rarely made financial decisions on my own. My experience with budgeting was both limited and unproductive. Once on my own, however, I determined to handle my new life responsibly and with care. Necessity (and a little fear) propelled me to seek out wise counsel. I learned how to make good financial choices, starting with a monthly budget for my life.

I rarely make purchases, including for travel, that aren't part of my budget. Planning in advance how much I expect to spend, both in preparation for the trip and when I'm on the road, creates more space and time to devote to wonder and joy instead of financial stress and anxiety.

For the past 30+ years, I have planned travel for myself, family, friends, an entire girls travel soccer team, and, more recently, for clients. Road trips, family vacations, girls' weekends, trips to Italy—I love it all. I even find joy in plotting out the budget. It's a puzzle of sorts, and I'm always up for a puzzle. One common denominator in all types of travel is that, almost always, the cost is a little more than expected. No matter how careful the plan or its implementation, the unforeseen happens, and it almost always costs more!

My hope here is to help you alleviate as much of the unexpected costs as possible by sharing what I've learned along the way. I will not tell you how to manage your money. What I can offer, however, are tips and tools learned in my years of budgeting for road-tripping adventure.

To Save or Not to Save

Whether you have plenty of cash on hand now or you're starting at zero, I highly recommend devoting time to planning what you can afford to spend on your trip, and then, if necessary, saving up before you go.

As a starting point, consider which of the following currently applies to you:

a. I need to save up before I can travel.

b. I have enough "play" money without saving.

c. I'm charging everything to a credit card and paying later.

d. I haven't thought about it.

Knowing how you intend to fund your trip leads to realistic expectations. If you answered "d," no worries! This section will help you get there. And no surprise . . . "c" is probably not anyone's best option unless you determine in advance how much you plan to spend and pay off your card in full at the end of the month. While you may feel carefree on the road, all that joy and wonder will disappear so much more quickly when your credit card statement comes due.

Be deliberate. Think through your options and decide in advance how you plan to fund your fun! If you need to save, be patient and offer grace to yourself in the process.

How Much?

For first-time road-trippers, it can be tricky to feel confident about how much you'll need to finance your adventure. You won't do a perfect job of it, but if you're used to budgeting at home, you know that with each passing month you get better at predicting your spending. Before we begin crunching numbers, consider the three primary areas of road-trip expenditure.

1. Pre-trip planning
2. In-trip purchases
3. Emergency fund

Devoting time and a bit of research to each of these areas in advance will lead to a confident projection of total spending for the trip. As we work through them, you will undoubtedly want to add your own thoughts and personal needs to the list.

Remember my note about the different planning essentials intertwining? Budgeting is a prime example. It's difficult to dig too deeply into your budget planning without considering your plan for meals, lodging, packing, and even safety. Individual chapters devoted to each will detail the specifics of planning, costs, and saving hacks. For now, pay attention to the big ideas!

A note of encouragement before we dive in. You don't have to spend thousands of dollars to be a wonder-seeker! There are infinite ways to keep costs down and save money during the planning process as well as mid-trip. You can be frugal without sacrificing adventure and safety. Look for suggestions and tips in the upcoming chapters!

Pre-trip Purchases

Before we jump ahead to the trip itself, there are plenty of pre-planning budget considerations. For your first road trip, it's likely you'll be in the market for some bigger item (or items!) before you pack the car. While I'm all for borrowing what you can, sometimes you may want to invest in having your own gear. The chapters on food, lodging, and packing will dive into the details, but as you work through your budget, make a note of those items you know you need to acquire in advance.

If you can't afford "all the things" before you travel, determine what you really need versus what you're able to forego or work around for now. My strategy has been to prioritize the essentials and buy one or two larger items each year. It's taken me quite a while to build my inventory, and in most cases I have chosen to purchase quality items that will stand the test of time. While my wish list is never completely depleted, over time I have built up a more than adequate collection of road-tripping essentials.

And before you jump online or head out shopping, don't be afraid to see what hacks there may be as an alternative to spending a significant amount on certain items. YouTube, as well as travel blogs, are incredible resources to mine ideas, especially if money is tight. A trip to check out your local thrift stores, perusing Facebook Marketplace, Craig's List, yard sales and other secondhand options may lead to treasure also.

When I first began driving long distances, my budget was squeaky tight. I wanted to give camping a try as that seemed most cost-effective, but I didn't want to invest in a tent, partly because I wasn't convinced I was ready to camp alone. (Now I highly recommend it!) That first year, I made no significant purchases because I couldn't afford anything extra. Instead, I tricked out my SUV to some extent and slept in it. I found websites that provided ideas about how to attach screening to windows for circulation while keeping the bugs out, and how to pack everything I needed yet leave enough room to stretch out and sleep in the back. I have incredible memories of these nights, and they represent some of my earliest moments finding freedom and wonder on the road. However, I vowed to save enough money to purchase a tent and air mattress before hitting the road again!

At this point, you may not know what purchases you actually need to make before you depart. (You may, however, know that under no circumstances will you ever need a tent!) It will become clearer as you plan. Know this—you'll probably need to stop at a Walmart within 24 hours of leaving home. I almost always do, no matter how well I plan. Don't worry about not getting it all right the first time, because you won't!

Below, I'll share a few bigger items I've budgeted for over the years. I've kept the categories broad for now, and we will look at each more closely in the chapters ahead. You'll note that not all are tangible items. Among them are expenditures necessary for health and safety. Additionally, some are one-time purchases, while others need to be replaced occasionally or are recurring expenses (like hiking shoes and taking Lexi to the vet before we go). Yours may be wildly different, depending on your style of travel.

- Clothing and shoes
- Coolers
- Car maintenance
- Packing containers
- Tech items
- Pet-related prep (if you travel with your pooch!)
- Camping gear
- Hiking gear

One other consideration regarding pre-travel expenses: while food and lodging tend to be two of the largest in-trip expenditures, most of both are often paid for in advance.

As you manage your cash flow between pre-trip and in-trip expenses, keep these two facts in mind.

- **Food:** Meal and snack planning means buying groceries before you go. This is a wonderful way to keep your total food costs down as it curbs the need to eat out often, but you'll have a hefty grocery bill prior to leaving.

- **Lodging:** Reservations for Airbnb, Vrbo, campgrounds, and some hotels typically require paying when you book, or at least paying a portion when you make the reservation.

Be sure to factor these into your overall budget:

- More expensive items you may need to purchase prior to your departure date

- Prepaid food and lodging

In-Trip Purchases

While you can easily manage your spending prior to your adventure, it can be a little trickier once you're on the road, especially the first time. How do you know how much you'll spend on food? Entertainment? Gas? It is possible to set reasonably accurate expectations! Once you consider the suggestions here and conduct a bit of your own research, you'll be able to confidently create a reasonable budget for what you plan to spend during your adventure.

How you travel will dictate the areas for which you

need to budget. For most road trips, the biggest outpouring of money is for "the big three"—food, lodging, and gas. However, if you're planning a theme trip to see concerts in each destination city or an abundance of Major League Baseball games, then significant funds will be allotted for tickets. Maybe you imagine finding every small-town bookstore and adding to your collection of first edition Agatha Christies or your destination is a lavish spa where you plan to indulge for several days. Whatever it is, budget for it!

Categories

1. Food
2. Lodging
3. Gas/tolls
4. Entry fees
5. Keepsakes
6. Additional fun!
7. Emergencies

Food

It's worthwhile to consider your eating needs and habits in advance. Chances are you'll be spending a lot of time in the car, and depending on your choice of routes, eating options may vary wildly. In addition to whatever pre-trip planning you may do, be sure to reasonably estimate how much you'll eat out, the need to replenish at the grocery store, or even visits to coffee shops, wineries, breweries, or other similar establishments you'd like to enjoy!

Lodging

Whether your trip is for a weekend or a month, deciding

where you'll lay your head at night affects your budget more than any other factor. You can sleep in your car in a Walmart parking lot for free (more on that gem in the accommodations chapter) or spoil yourself utterly at a Four Seasons for an average of $500 a night. I feel confident that most of us will find a happy place between the two! Investing time to research locations and weigh your options will allow you to calculate a reasonable expectation for your accommodations budget. Hotel and Airbnb prices vary substantially depending on location, as do campground fees for tents and cabins. Feel free to peek ahead at the chapter on lodging if you need specific ideas for every style of travel and budget!

Gas and Tolls

Depending on the length of your trip, gasoline can become a huge expense. Prices may fluctuate from month to month and from state to state. Generally speaking, southern and less populated midwestern states boast cheaper gas prices, while traveling in the Northeast Corridor or the West will cost you significantly more per gallon. It's easy to find the average per-state prices online, and I love the Gas Buddy app on my phone for locating gas stations and prices when I'm on the road.

My philosophy of road-tripping involves steering clear of highways in most situations, but there are inevitably days when I find the nearest interstate or turnpike and just GO. Similar to gas prices, tolls vary from state to state and road to road. Since Covid, most toll roads are completely automated. It's worth investigating in advance how you will be billed, what brand of electronic toll collections are used on your routes, and if you can pay cash as you go.

If you plan to cover a lot of territory, do your research in advance so you have realistic expectations. It really adds up!

Entry Fees

This may be a broad category, but chances are it applies to most everyone in some form. Consider the places you plan to visit that will require an entry fee of some sort. The range is wide! Whether you're driving into a national or state park, spending a day at a music festival or county fair, or riding a car ferry, you'll likely need to purchase a ticket for something. If you're heading out to visit a variety of Major League Baseball parks, prices may be significant for good seats, while ferrying across a river in Virginia may cost only a few dollars. Chances are you can research prices for most of these activities, but build a little extra into your budget as there are always surprises!

Keepsakes

Whether you buy gifts for friends and family or trinkets and keepsakes for yourself, be sure to pad your budget with room for extra goodies. It can be easy for me to blow my budget here, depending upon how much I shop or if a particular location or unique item resonates with me. A specific, set figure in my budget protects me from myself!

Spontaneous Fun!

Some things you just will not think of until they happen. That's certainly part of the wonder of a road trip. In many cases, wonder is free of charge, but occasionally you'll want to explore somewhere unexpected. I have incurred unexpected "fun" expenses in the form of a kayak or paddleboard rental or an impulse stop at a thermal spring or museum I hadn't planned to investigate. Often, though, my extra expenses go toward a fun evening out or a bit of a splurge on a hotel room. Padding my budget somewhat for these fun additions allows me to enjoy a little indulgence without the guilt!

It's quite possible your unique adventure will include additional expenses I have not included here. Be sure to add any other categories that require consideration for your particular plan.

Emergency Funds

It can be scary when things go wrong, and occasionally something will—you can count on it. In some cases, problems come with price tags. Whether it's a fender bender or a lost debit card, at the very least you'll be inconvenienced, but being in an unexpected situation with no ability to pay can be downright frightening. You can't anticipate every circumstance, but budgeting in advance for the unexpected always pays off. Think of it as an insurance policy—you may or may not need it, but it will provide peace of mind as you wander. And if you don't need it, you come home with extra money for your next road trip!

When you create your budget, be sure to include a line item for emergencies. Some of this will be cash, but not all. In the chapter on safety, we will discuss scenarios regarding lost or stolen money, credit cards, and phones. For the moment, our attention is solely on the budgeting aspect of potential emergencies.

There are two varieties of emergency funds. Hopefully you won't need either, but plan for both.

1. Keep some money (I suggest between $100 and $300) hidden in your car for emergencies. An alternative is to store away a smaller amount of cash along with an extra credit, debit, or prepaid Visa card. A good rule of thumb is to have enough

money for a hotel room, a meal, and the purchase of a disposable phone and/or a tank of gas.

2. For bigger issues such as major car problems, it's best to have enough saved in your bank account to cover expenses as opposed to carrying significant amounts of cash with you. It's likely you won't need to access it, but there's peace of mind in knowing you have the emergency fund if it becomes necessary.

Several summers ago, I had planned for a week-long meandering return from a western road trip. A portion of the drive included cruising a few hundred miles down the Great River Road along the mighty Mississippi. The plan was for Lexi the Golden and I to camp as many nights as possible.

An unexpected and intense heatwave settled heavily on the midwestern states, dispelling any thoughts of sleeping in a tent. Incredible humidity in South Dakota, Minnesota, Wisconsin, Missouri, and Kentucky led to evenings that "cooled off" only into the mid 80s. It was just too hot. I tried to locate Airbnbs as we headed east but found very little available and nothing very cost effective. And so, Lexi and I had no other choice but to stay in hotels the entire way across the Midwest. As wonderful as the air conditioning proved to be, I hadn't budgeted many hundreds of extra dollars for the pleasure of cool air. Adding pet fees on top of room fees to my credit card made for an unexpectedly expensive week and put a bit of a damper on the final days of my trip.

I learned the hard way to plan for missteps and ensure my emergency account is funded. No doubt I will encounter unplanned exploits for as long as I travel. Hopefully very few of them will be costly, though it's likely my emergency fund will take a significant hit at some point. There's great peace in knowing the money is there should it happen.

Payment Plans

In many ways, we are fortunate to have a plethora of options to access our money. Beyond the obvious cash or credit/debit choices, we can now tap into PayPal, Apple Pay, Zelle, or Venmo. No doubt even more alternatives are on the ever-changing horizon. Some of these apps can connect to credit cards, while others withdraw money directly from a checking account. If you anticipate utilizing any of these payment methods, be certain they are set up properly in advance and that you know what accounts they are connected to. Keep in mind—if you are in locations with little to no cell service, you will be unable to utilize the payment apps on your phone!

Also consider that not every place you visit may take credit cards. When you travel in unfamiliar locations, it's definitely best to have options. If you are traveling to Amish Country, for example, many stores and services are cash or check only. Additionally, you may encounter toll roads and ferries that only take cash, or a gas station whose credit card access connection isn't working. It happens! Consider that if you lose your phone, many of those alternative methods of payment become null and void.

I've experienced quite a few memorable moments with money while traveling—now fun stories, though all were unnerving at the time! The most recent episode can only be described as a "small town situation," and while it was hardly scary, it proved a solid reminder of two important lessons: 1) always carry some cash, and 2) there are wonderfully trusting and honest people in the world.

Heading into the mountains of northern Pennsylvania, I stopped near a tiny town for gas at a very local station. It offered no name other than "Service Garage" stenciled in the front window along with the phone number, nor did it advertise any particular brand of gasoline. Just "regular" or "diesel." With no "pay at the pump" option, I filled my tank and entered the small lobby to pay with my card.

"Machines are down," I was told when I entered. The guy behind the counter informed me that he could not run credit or debit cards but that I could use the ATM to withdraw cash, as I had none on me. Great plan, but no such luck. Turned out the ATM operated on the same system as the credit card scanners, so I was left with literally no way to pay for $47 worth of fuel. Two local gentlemen stood in line ahead of me with the same conundrum, though I was clearly the only stranger in the mix. These fellas were well known to one another.

Behind-the-counter-guy thought quickly and triumphantly declared, "No problem!" pulling out scrap paper and writing our names and the amounts owed on slips of paper. He proceeded to pop them into the cash drawer, saying, "Just stop by next time you drive by. We'll keep the IOU in the drawer until then." Wonder found in a trusting soul in a middle-of-nowhere fill-up station.

That trip was short enough that I hadn't really considered it a road trip, but rather a quick weekend to my family's farm in the mountains. However, it served as a gentle reminder to devote more attention to payment options before I leave home, and I was grateful to learn that lesson pain-free! When

I stopped at the station on the return trip, my guy was not on duty. The owner of the service station listened to my story and showed genuine surprise as I handed over my $47!

Whether you are a seasoned money manager or contemplating your first budget, investing time and a bit of research in advance of your road trip will ensure fewer financial surprises and a lot more peace.

You may find yourself in other unplanned (and costly) situations during your time on the road. I've been there a few times, and while I've learned from those mistakes, chances are I'll create new blunders in the future. There's grace for all of it, and there's no earthly way to know what's around the bend. That very feeling is why I love road-tripping. We're not promised an adventure with no glitches, and the joy far outweighs the messes!

Additional budgeting tips, resources,
and information can be found at:
www.wonderbingtravel.com/book-resources

Chapter 12

Time and Distance

Although each day contains 24 hours, each single one presents a unique set of circumstances. Don't try to force-fit today into yesterday's mold. Instead, ask Me to open your eyes, so you can find all I have prepared for you in this precious day of life.

—Sarah Young, *Jesus Calling*[1]

Each day spent on the road will be unlike any other—an unrepeatable gift. At home, when my world feels redundant, I need frequent reminders to embrace each moment. As I adventure, however, uniqueness is baked into the pursuit of wonder. New places and people, singular sights and sounds, uncovering and discovering and seeing anew every day. What about you? What is God preparing for your wonder-seeking days? What will you discover as you open your mind and heart to every precious new unrepeatable gift? I wonder!

The mysteries around each bend, the not knowing until it happens, are indeed part of the wonder. You just want to be ready. Ready for both the tiny moments and the ones that shift the earth beneath you—each ultimately changing the way you see yourself and the world.

I believe there is freedom in structure, in having a plan. Investing time to create a strategy for each of the essentials of road-tripping doesn't slow you down or hinder you. Quite the opposite! Asking and answering the big questions in advance builds confidence for the day-to-day. You'll worry less and enhance your ability to experience freedom on the road.

With each chapter, I hope the excitement for planning your own adventure is building, along with your confidence. Hopefully our budget discussion cemented some decisions relative to the length of your adventure (time) as well as the miles you'll cover (distance). While you may not yet be able to accurately predict exact dates and miles, you likely know if you're plotting for a couple of days and lower mileage, or something significantly longer. With that main foundational piece in place, we can explore how to manage timing and distance for the day-to-day, thus bringing you one step closer to packing the car and beginning your journey!

Do a Little Math

Determining the total days and miles of your trip provides a springboard for you to move forward and plan all the fun stuff! Let's confirm that the distance and time it will take to travel to your destination(s) sync with your overall plan for the length of your adventure. There are two ways to approach this. One using an estimated number of hours spent driving per day, and the other based on miles driven. Additionally, you may recall that navigation is one of our road-tripping essentials. That overlaps here as we confirm time and distance. In the next chapter we will delve into all the details of navigating your trip. For now, let's keep it simple.

Time-Based

Use an online navigation tool, such as Google Maps or Apple Maps, to calculate the approximate total hours of driving time required to navigate from your starting place to your furthest destination. While you can certainly use your phone, I find that using google.com/maps on my laptop provides more detail and clearer visuals.

Keep in mind that if you plan to skirt the highways, your driving time will be significantly longer. Most online mapping systems allow you to choose a "no highway" option, which provides a more accurate estimate. If you plan to go off course completely, or diverge on various side trips, be sure to add those mini-digressions and destinations into your total. Again, I love Google's map site for this, as it allows you to plot up to a total of ten destinations.

Divide your total driving time each way by the number of days you'll be driving. Be sure to count driving days only and leave out any extra days you may spend exploring in stops along the way or at your destination.

Here's a working example, though depending on your personality you're either going to love it or skip it entirely. Only use it if it helps!

1. I plan an eight-day trip from Pittsburgh to Memphis.
2. The fastest highway route indicates a little over 11 hours of driving each way.
3. If I choose the most direct "no highway" option

on Google, it quickly jumps to 16.5 hours. That's a significant difference and important for planning.

4. If I plan to arrive in Memphis later in the day on day three, spend three nights there, and depart the morning of day six, that allows for 5 days on the road plus my arrival day in Memphis.

5. If I choose to drive the highways, that results in just a little over 3.5 hours on the road per day.

6. If I stay off the main roads, my driving time jumps to 5.5 hours each day.

Distance-Based

Alternatively, you can use mileage as your guide. The shortest and fastest route from Pittsburgh is listed as 771 miles, and the most direct no-highway option is almost identical at 780. The time, however, is drastically different, as we computed above (11 versus 16.5 hours.). In this case, factoring mileage alone isn't very helpful in making a decision.

Leave Time to Wonder

If you choose to invest in time to wonder along the way, make room for creativity! As an example, my planning involves looking at a bigger picture. (And a bigger map!) As I plot a trip from Pittsburgh to Memphis, I don't see just the direct route, highways or no highways. I see West Virginia, Ohio, Kentucky, and Tennessee, and plenty of opportunities to explore significantly along the way. I often explore 50 miles or more away from any direct route and will typically create my own course. You absolutely have the freedom to abandon the predetermined computing of mapping software and let your mind wander into wonder!

There is endless room to adjust how you plot this out. If you discover the math reveals more driving per day than you initially planned for, play with your options until you find one that works for you. Maybe you drive more days than originally planned, but cover fewer miles each day, leaving more time for meandering, spontaneous stops, etc. You can adjust your route, make up time on a highway if you're heading through more desolate areas, or even leave home a day or two early if it fits your schedule. Be openminded and willing to adjust!

Our upcoming chapter on navigation will explore this in detail. If a more complicated route feels overwhelming for now, keep it simple! The basic Point A to Point B calculation offers a workable starting point.

Occasionally I have to stop mid-planning and either walk away or take a deep breath because I can wade a little too deeply into the minutiae. I have to remind myself to lighten up just a bit. Sarah Young provides another wonderful nugget of advice that speaks to me loudly and clearly. While she wasn't referring specifically to travel planning, the sentiment fits perfectly! Again, she speaks with Jesus' voice.

Instead of trying to fit this day into a preconceived mold, relax and be on the lookout for what I am doing. This mindset will free you to enjoy me and to find what I have planned for you to do. This is far better than trying to make things go according to your own plan.

—Sarah Young, *Jesus Calling*[2]

Again, freedom. Freedom to relax and enjoy the process. Freedom in knowing you are ultimately not in control of these details. Freedom to keep your eyes wide open, looking out for what God has planned for each day.

Daily Travel Time

In our Personal Peace chapter (Chapter 8), we explored the importance of setting up our days in a way that provides peace in both our hearts and our heads. I shared my specific list of daily needs on the road and suggested you determine your own. Now we are ready to infuse those spiritual and practical "daily dos" into the bigger picture of each day.

As you plot the miles and time you plan to spend exploring, break your planning into two parts—

1. How and when you wish to begin and end each day.
2. The amount of time and miles traveled in the middle.

Every day will be unique, but having a general strategy will help keep you centered. Baselines are just suggestions, though. In many cases, wonder doesn't pay much attention to the clock!

In the Beginning, and the End

A significant measure of your peace, contentment, and confidence will be a direct result of how and when you begin and end each day on the road. You know yourself better than anyone. Trust that. Also, this part isn't complicated! I'll provide the reasoning for my own approach, and then you craft what works for you. Creating your own routine with clarity about your needs will help chart the larger scope of your daily adventuring, so be honest with yourself as you work through this.

As I shared previously, my basic rule of thumb is to be on the road between 9:00 and 10:00 in the morning and stop for the night between 5:00 and 7:00. It's taken me a while to learn that sticking to this on most occasions is in my best interest, and I know from plenty of experience that it works for me. Here's why:

- **I crave a flexible structure.** I know joy and contentment in my world are more about Jesus than my schedule, but there's no doubt that some structure helps me feel settled and at peace when I'm traveling.

  My driving window has plenty of time built in for wonder. My plan is rarely, if ever, to drive the entire day. Depending on how much ground I'm trying to cover, I can stop to explore, hike, wander through a town, have a picnic lunch, etc.

  Providing myself with a window of time at both the front and back end of each day also provides wiggle room for the unexpected and helps ensure I don't make a big mess of things!

- **I'm an introvert at heart.** I thrive when I can begin and end each day slowly and with some purpose. Lexi and I are early risers, and if I'm camping, I love the early morning quiet. There's also a period of time to enjoy my morning routine, take a hike, and strike the campsite before I get going.

  If I'm staying in a small town, there's plenty of time built in for exploring in the mornings and evenings when things tend to be quieter. Time to pop into a bookstore, enjoy local coffee or a glass of wine, and walk around to truly get the feel of the place. I can talk to people if I choose to, but just as easily wander under the radar.

Traveling in the summer can be uncomfortably hot, and the loveliest times of the day are in the cool of the early mornings. For this reason, I try to start each day with a run, hike, or walk when it's a bit cooler.

- **Practical (and magical) evenings.** Settling in early in the evenings serves me well on many fronts.

  o I'm a curious person, and I don't like arriving at my destination in the dark. It's important to me to have time to check things out, walk around, and get the lay of the land.

  o If I'm camping, I hate setting up in a rush and in the dark.

  o Safety: Arriving in daylight is always safer!

  o Time for dinner: If we're camping, then there's time to get dinner in the daylight. If I'm headed out, there's plenty of time to scope things out.

  o Showing up later in the evening also means I probably won't rest as well. Getting good sleep when you're on the road is key!

  o I don't want to miss anything, so driving in the dark just doesn't work for me.

  o Some of my favorite moments on a road trip are those quiet moments in front of a campfire, moon rising, book in hand and dog at my feet. And just about as lovely, snuggled up in some cute rental home or hotel with that same dog!

Whether you find a few nuggets to relate to here or your ideas are vastly different, give some thought to a loose structure for how and when you'll start and end your days. Jot down estimated starting and ending times that will meet your needs. This will provide more confidence for savoring all those golden hours of wonder in the middle. As you gain experience, you'll naturally make adjustments until you hit that peaceful sweet spot where you've established structure and made space to follow what beckons you in exactly those measures that please you best.

The Golden Hours

Once you get comfortable with the time you build into the front and back end of each day, you're left with all those delicious golden hours in between. On a road trip, the "golden hour" isn't reserved for those precious minutes before the sun slips behind the sea or the mountain. It's not a solitary sixty minutes at all, but the hours-long treasure of all that wide-eyed travel time each day. This is the heart of the road trip! And the ultimate setting for freedom and wonder.

If you're even a little daunted, concerned that all those hours of freedom may generate more questions than answers, it's okay! If it feels overwhelming—also okay! The chapters ahead are full of ideas and strategies for making the most of each day.

Let's start with this. Remember you're planning a road trip seeking wonder in God's creation, not building a battleship. Relax. Don't be afraid to make decisions. Yes, weird things will happen. Mistakes will be made. It won't all go as planned. Trust that God has led you to this point, and you will never be lost or alone. There is no one correct formula for how you plan your days. Stay true to your instincts and your personal sense of adventuring. Just keep the pursuit of wonder at the heart of each path you take.

Ultimately it will be up to you to curate the specifics of your trip. It's your unique journey. Your confidence will continue to grow as we consider the details of navigation, lodging and food, etc. For the moment, let me offer a few big-picture suggestions. They won't keep you from experiencing pitfalls or days that leave you scratching your head and wondering how *that* happened, but perhaps I can provide encouragement, save you a little stress, and stave off a few of your anxious thoughts before they take hold.

The most significant piece of advice I can provide is one I continue to relearn at least once on each journey: **Don't cram too much into one day**—*the joy starts to seep out of the cracks, wonder becomes less obvious (especially if you have to speed past tempting places because there's now no time!). Frankly, overdoing it on the road starts to reflect shades of the busy life you've left in the rear-view mirror, which can be both disheartening and exhausting.*

Be mentally prepared to ditch everything some days. Stuff happens! I've encountered nights when it's too hot to follow through on a camping plan, a trip when I arrived at a completely flooded campground in the middle of nowhere, a two-day span when Lexi couldn't walk after an injury, and massive wildfires which caused me to reroute hundreds of miles from my intended destination.

Every trip I've taken has required a "Plan B" at some point. In every case, God knew. Plans changed, and wonder continued albeit in a slightly different form than I originally imagined. God's plans are so much better than mine. Remember you are seeking wonder in His world and in His creation. Be open to all that God puts in your path.

Each day is a one-time offer, non-refundable and with an immediate expiration date. As years pile up in the rear view, the truth of this becomes more tangible. I treasure the freedom to explore—to revel in new experiences, even though some days on the road are intimidating, exhausting, and not what I had imagined. I learn as I go, and there are times when the wisdom and wonder aren't revealed until after the fact, when I'm safely tucked in for the night, replaying the day, choosing to revel in it as gift.

You don't need to have it all figured out today. Turn the page when you're ready and delve into the rest of our road-tripping essentials. Remember they all work together, complimenting one another and intertwining.

> **Additional tips, resources, and information**
> **on planning for time and distance**
> **can be found at:**
> **www.wonderbingtravel.com/book-resources**

Chapter 13

Navigation

Britannica's online dictionary defines navigation as "the act, activity, or process of finding the way to get to a place . . ." The "finding the way" part resonates with me. I love that it hints at endless possibility and multiple right answers. After all, there are so many ways to get from Point A to Point B!

I realize this last statement either thrills or horrifies you. No doubt the topic of navigation strikes fear in some hearts. Perhaps it's because the scary monster previously keeping you from planning a road trip strongly resembles a map or a GPS. Or the idea of navigating exposes the vulnerabilities of feeling unmoored as you imagine yourself lost and directionless. Or maybe figuring it all out just feels overwhelming.

It was easy enough to revel in grand adventure dreams as they flashed joyfully through your brain, but as you let your mind move into the practicalities of actually determining how to get from Point A to Point B, you slam the proverbial brakes, fearfully rushing back to your comfy couch. You love the idea of wandering with purpose but are afraid of stumbling aimlessly, and you're just not sure you can manage it alone. If this is you, I see you, and you can do this.

Whether plotting your course instills a bit of terror in your soul, or you're at the other end of the spectrum and dying to get on with it, thinking through both the big and small considerations of navigation will help you avoid plenty of bumps in the road ahead. This pillar of the planning process connects to seeking wonder more than any other! And like most of the scary monsters under the bed, shedding some light on them tends to make them all but disappear.

Navigating as an Essential Piece

I share unabashedly that navigating might just be my favorite essential of planning a road trip. It's where the practical aspects of strategizing collide with romance and adventure. The end result? A mapped-out design for wonder. It's also the payoff for investing in the framework of the trip. At this point, we've poured the proverbial foundation and the framing is complete. You've created a hard-won infrastructure that now frees you to impart your own personality into the project. To design a path that you love! Making decisions about how you'll navigate through your journey will be guided by all those ideas you cultivated back in the Treasure Map chapter. It's time to pull them out and finalize some plans!

As we move forward, we'll divide our discussion into two separate phases of navigation: pre-trip and en route. Much of your course will be mapped out as part of "pre-trip navigation," which we will dig into first. The inevitable second stage unfolds on the road. Knowing your proclivities for the level of planning that makes you comfortable will drive how you balance the two. Most likely you'll fall into a pattern where you make the bigger decisions in advance and the smaller day-to-day ones en route. If you feel you'll be more self-assured mapping as much as possible in advance and securing a plan for each day, perfect! Do what makes you feel comfortably adventurous!

Pre-trip Navigation

It's time to bring out your treasure map to determine which pieces will fit into your adventure!

Back to the Treasure Map

Now that we've worked through the essentials of time and distance and budget, you can look at your treasure map in a new light. If you haven't transferred your ideas to a map yet, do it! It will make for a much richer visual as we progress. You can highlight, add tiny sticky notes, or if your map is hanging up, pin away!

If you breezed through Chapter 5, unsure of where this all would lead you, take some time to go back now and compile your lists of interesting stopovers and destinations. The Treasure Map chapter is full of suggestions about where to mine for ideas if you're a bit stuck. Once you have a pile of possibilities, you're that much closer to real encounters with wonder, ready to transition from ideas to itinerary.

More recently, we've considered the planning pillars of time and distance, a budget, and the big picture of planning a solo road trip. All that intention means you're ready to take a more thoughtful approach to your treasure map now.

While the Treasure Map chapter focused on dreaming, our next task is to plot those wonder-filled possibilities into your prospective route.

The Case for Maps

Effectively creating a road trip involves visual planning. Unlike a normal day of hopping in your car to drive directly and expeditiously to a singular destination, developing a route with a mix of planned and unplanned stops requires envisioning it first on paper or screen.

In my completely unscientific opinion, there are two kinds of people: those who obsessively love maps and those who are terrified of them. I'll concede there may be a few folks riding the middle, but not many. Thus, for some, maps hold no mystery. They're just confusing, impossibly difficult-to-fold hunks of paper full of lines and numbers. To me, though, any map is a treasure map. Maps are the visual key to unlock the grandest of adventures. They inspire confidence as well as curiosity. That squiggly lines and a few words and numbers can accurately indicate how to precisely navigate makes all the sense in the world to me. I am a map nerd.

I love spreading out the paper US map. It's a wonderful way to begin dreaming through any upcoming adventure, and over the years I have also invested in maps of each state I've traversed, not to mention maps of cities, national and state parks, and hiking trails—all of these are part of my literal rite of passage for every trip I take. While I depend on GPS and my phone for a lot of moment-to-moment in-trip navigation, it is the spreading out of the paper onto the dining room table, highlighter in hand, that excites me more than any other singular moment in planning a road trip. That's when I can see it all in front of me. That's when it gets real.

If you're nodding your head as you read along, you need no further encouragement. However, if map-reading sounds scary and unnecessary, I hope you can power through this bit and come out on the other side with less rancor (and a little bit of hope) in your heart. And a note to the millennials here—I see you rolling your eyes. "Like, you want me to hold (let alone fold) a paper map?" I know. I hear you. But there are things that your GPS and all the magic apps just can't provide. Technology plays a wonderfully huge role in navigation, just not at this juncture. Give maps a chance!

I'd like to make both a spiritual and practical case for the absolute need for a map at this stage of your wonder planning. Yes, spiritual. Read on as we unpack it!

The Spiritual Side

Maps provide us with a geographic sense of our place in the world. They offer an irrefutable visual that connects our smaller selves to the world at large. They literally put us in our place.

In the great American classic *Our Town*, Thornton Wilder creates a moment of wonder for young Rebecca Gibbs as she endeavors to place her own small life within the cosmic universe. As she and her brother George enjoy the moonlight of a New Hampshire evening, she shares her amazement at the address on the envelope of a letter a friend had received.

He wrote Jane a letter and on the envelope the address was like this: It said: Jane Crofut; The Crofut Farm; Grover's Corners; Sutton County; New Hampshire; United States of America... Continent of North America; Western Hemisphere; the

> *Earth; the Solar System; the Universe; the Mind of God—that's what it said on the envelope.*
>
> —*Our Town*, Act I

Wilder makes his point clear: the world is vast—we are but a tiny speck, not only in the universe but in the Mind of God. I would like to add that you bear His image, created purposely and specifically, every hair on your head both counted and known. What a paradox, to all at once feel so small and yet so alive and completely known. How much you are loved and cared for by our heavenly Father!

In the visual context of finding yourself on paper, it's no wonder opening a map can bring on some anxiety. But let it bring joy as well. You are fully known by Him. You will never be lost or out of His sight, and He has created this blue ball of earth and water as a way for us to seek and find the wonder of Him.

Practically Speaking

Spread out your map. If it's immediately overwhelming, start by marking your own location. You know where you are! A map provides us with a realistic look at what we can accomplish in the space of a trip. If you're geographically challenged, take a moment to acclimate yourself and your proximity to other known places. Get a sense of what's reasonably close and what's just too much for this trip.

Mark your beginning and ending points, and any other known waypoints. Consider all those wonder-filled locations that you've been pinning and highlighting. Add any that haven't yet found their way to your map and set aside those that no longer make sense this time around. Creating this visual for where you're headed is the best way to see what's out there. Now you have a picture of how to move forward.

If you have plenty of options already, bravo! The hard part is choosing what fits best with your time and schedule when you want to do it all. If there are big open spaces on your map with areas you know little about, take a closer look to see if anything jumps out at you. I discovered Laura Ingalls Wilder's home in Mansfield, Missouri, as I planned a driving route to Colorado. It became a must-do stop on my way through, and I wouldn't have known about it if it weren't clearly marked on my state map of Missouri.

Maps also provide a great opportunity to see various road options. When using state maps, the detail is significantly finer than on a map of the whole country, which opens up possibilities to see smaller towns, lakes, streams, state and national parklands, historical places of interest, etc. Be sure to read the legend! Understanding the colors that indicate each type of road can be the difference between meandering on two-lane back roads versus paying your way across a state on turnpikes and toll roads.

Ultimately, maps help you visualize the big picture of your trip and ensure you're making reasonable decisions as you navigate. They also provide the comfort of knowing your place in the world, and like *Our Town's* Rebecca Webb, they offer plenty of perspective!

Take some time to work through all that we've discussed here. Spread out your map(s), mark all your potential stops and winnow it down until it feels both manageable and exciting! The rest of the chapter will help solidify things, so don't agonize over your plans. Feel the freedom to sit with this awhile and take your time. You'll get there in the end!

Planned Pauses

In your pre-planning, you will discover a few (or many) places you plan to spend time, whether it be an hour or an entire day. At this point, you may have plotted them out on your map, but there will no doubt be holes. Holes refer to broad stretches of space from one stop to the next with no plan. You may determine just to drive on through, but if you'd like further options, how to find them at this point? Fun research! I love this part of planning, and though I end up with more possibilities than I can ultimately enjoy, they help me chart my way through the days.

Here's an example of the "hole-filling" process taken from a trip several years back. After reading about the Great River Road in a travel book, I decided to explore a portion of it on my return trip from the West. The Great River Road follows the path of the Mississippi River from northern Minnesota all the way to the Gulf of Mexico for a total of almost 3,000 miles. For my part, I planned to drive just a few hundred miles in total, from La Crosse, Wisconsin, south to St. Louis, visiting river towns along the way.

While it helps to have a basic understanding of the area, this was all new territory for me. The entire road was the equivalent of a giant hole on my map. Searching for more information, I found a book on Amazon that was dedicated specifically to driving the Great River Road and discovered a website as well.

> *No matter where you may wander, someone has been there before you. Words have been written and photos have been taken.*

Once I pinpointed my main stops, I added Pinterest, Instagram, and Google to my list of places to search for specifics. As I learned more about the River Road, towns like Galena, Illinois, and Mark Twain's Hannibal, Missouri, leapt out at me and helped me firm up my plans. This is such a part of the adventure! I create inspiration boards on Pinterest for each trip and stockpile all the articles and posts I discover that pique my interest, knowing I'll need to sift through them as I finalize my plans for these intentional mini destinations.

Settling on the towns and other sights I planned to visit on the Great River Road took some time and research, but every bit I learned made the trip richer when I cruised south along the Mighty Mississippi that summer.

Knowing in advance where I plan to stop is a little like a security blanket. It provides comfort, but also the confidence to explore on a whim whenever something strikes me. Confidence, freedom, and wonder. The perfect combination for exploration!

The Full-Day Pause

On last summer's road trip, I knew I'd be heading from the Cleveland area north into Michigan to enjoy the Great Lakes and Michigan's Upper Peninsula. In the year prior to my trip, I remembered seeing a friend and her husband post photos from this amazing-looking spot called Mackinac Island. I did some research and decided it would be the perfect longer day stop.

Making the day work into my larger plan involved some online investigating: understanding a ferry schedule (to and from the island), scoping out the level of dog-friendliness, and then researching to get a feel for weather, activities, walkability, etc. All my research paid off.

The island is small, and we were able to walk everywhere. Lexi swam in Lake Huron, we enjoyed a gorgeous hike, ate two meals, and even accidentally witnessed a wedding on the beach. After enjoying incredible local ice cream as a final treat, we ferried back to our car and headed north to our campground, put up the tent, and enjoyed the sunset.

Based on my research I was able to create reasonable expectations. I planned to arrive on the island before noon, enjoy the main part of the day, and be on our way to the state park with the campsite set up before dark. All adventures were accomplished, there were plenty of unexpected moments of wonder, and we had a glorious day!

Mini Breaks

Typically, short stops involve towns or hikes I have scoped out on the map or in my online research of the areas I'm driving through. I incorporate them into the course of my driving and allow them to break up the day and ensure I'm experiencing a bit of the local flavor in the areas I pass through.

Inevitably some of these plans fall by the wayside on days where I've tried to do too much, the weather turns ugly, or something better pops up! Ultimately, I can't do everything, and that's okay. It's better to have a firm idea of the big navigation picture and trip as a whole and then prioritize the small stuff as I go. No need for panic or confusion if something doesn't fit into the day—just go on to the next. Flexible is fun!

As a seasoned road-tripper, I find myself preplanning fewer and fewer small stops. As my confidence level has increased over the years, I feel more comfortable letting some days unfold on their own. On my very first major solo road trip, however, I did plan out many of my mini-stops. The planning gave me confidence and helped me measure distances that worked for me each day. I tried not to over plan; every stop on that trip was leisurely and kept the blood pressure nice and low, including lunch with my college roommate in Lynchburg, Virginia, several hikes along Virginia's Skyline Drive and the Blue Ridge Parkway, a visit to Toccoa Falls in Georgia, and afternoons wandering around the beautiful little towns of Madison, Georgia, and Micanopy, Florida. I spent six days on the road driving from Northern Virginia to Islamorada, Florida, avoiding highways at every opportunity. It was a sweet, slow, wonder-filled week.

There was also a bounty of unplanned fun during those six days, mostly discovered in my time on back roads as I cut through the mountains, cruised through forgotten little southern towns, and gaped at the endless square miles of Florida orange groves. I remember not really being certain I wanted to arrive at my destination, as my time on the road had been filled with so much joy and adventure.

As you lean into your own planning, make a conscious effort not to overdo it! Too much research and information can easily lead you down a rabbit hole. There's a line between solid planning that puts the road firmly under your wheels and planning hijacked by excessive focus on detail, sucking the fun out of your adventure. Getting stuck in the minutiae leads to stress and anxiety, the antithesis of freedom and wonder. Remember the goal is to create a mix of deliberate planning to ensure confidence with plenty of uncharted opportunity for wonder-filled surprises. You've heard the expression, "I plan, God laughs"? It definitely applies to traveling!

Conclusion: Do what makes you comfortable and confident. The wonder will be waiting.

En Route Navigation

It's incredibly helpful to create a strategy for your road trip, a blueprint of sorts. But wonder typically isn't found in the blueprint. It's found in between the lines in the unexpected moments. In addition to mapping out the grand scheme, spontaneous adventuring awaits each day you drive—the hard left turn when you see a sign for an old antique market or a homemade ice cream shop. The choice to pull over and wade into the blue waters of a clear mountain stream or sink into the warm wide sand leading into the Atlantic. So much of the beauty and the wonder comes from the mystery of not knowing what you'll encounter with each passing mile. It really is the part of road-tripping that we tend to dream about, right? What might I see just around this next bend, and this one, and this one? Intoxicating and addicting!

Your decisions will be unique to you. This is a part of solo travel that is so beautiful. You make all the choices—go with your gut, do what you want, go where you feel led. No other opinion matters. For this reason, there's not much I can offer in terms of "how-to" lay out your en-route day. There are no instructions or guidelines! Instead, I will share a few tips as you prepare to begin each morning, and one truly blond moment I offer as a cautionary tale.

Tips to Prep for the Day

- **Keep Important Items within Reach:** When I pull out of the driveway, the seat next to me and its contents function in many ways as my co-pilot. They just don't eat my snacks! When we do a dive into packing, I'll share the particulars of what I've learned needs to be within arm's reach.

The short list of must-haves includes:

- o GPS (mine is built into my car)
- o Phone
- o Any map I could conceivably need
- o An old-school folder where I've printed out info regarding each leg of my trip

There will be times when the phone just doesn't do the job, or, if you have a car with built-in GPS, there are moments when you'll be without any kind of signal. Maps matter, as does printed access to reservation numbers, addresses, etc. I keep any relevant paperwork or technology within easy reach, and if I have an initial destination, I plug it into my phone and turn off the "highway" option. I take a few moments to pray, head in the direction of my first intended route, take a deep breath, relax, and open my eyes. I don't want to miss a thing.

- **Think a Day Ahead:** Devote a little time each evening or early morning to sketch out the day in front of you. A poor night of sleep or bad weather may impact your original plan, or perhaps the reality of time and distance will be different than expected. There are innumerable reasons for making adjustments! Ultimately it takes being mid-trip to understand how each day flows.

  Look at the map to see what's between you and your next night of sleep. Invest a little time in research. Look for trails to hike, interesting towns, historic or funky places of interest, festivals nearby, etc. Whatever interests you! Now that you have the lay of the land, you'll feel more confident and have a clearer picture of what fits into your day of impending adventure!

- **Pay Attention to Signs!** Perhaps obvious, but it's easy to daydream and spend time looking at everything except the words as you go cruising down the road. Especially when you're off the beaten path, you'll encounter signs directing you toward interesting landmarks that your map and GPS never revealed. I've stumbled upon plenty of unexpected wonder simply by reading what's in front of me and turning on a whim.

- **Take Brain (and Body) Breaks:** If you get overwhelmed at any point, don't hesitate to hop on a highway to make up time or find a comfortable place to regroup. Find a park where you can take a walk and rest for a bit, a coffee shop to refuel. Or on a longer trip, you may need to spend an extra night somewhere to catch up on sleep and truly relax.

One of the things that I've struggled with in the past is sticking to my "schedule." I've let it wear me out at times, and I ceased having fun because of the growing tension threatening to overtake me. In those moments, since my version of a road trip is based on freedom and wonder, I've felt guilty for not being true to my intentions. I have since learned how to pace myself, but sometimes I still bite off more than I can chew. If you do, there's grace for that. Offer that grace to yourself, take a break, and move on when you're ready!

- **Don't Trade in Your Brain for a GPS:** Our GPS systems have become necessary and incredibly helpful tools, but be careful not to exchange them for your brain.

This exact mistake led to one of the most clueless, ridiculous blunders of my road-tripping life. And this is coming from someone who claims to have a stellar built-in sense of direction.

A Very Blond Moment

One autumn evening, Lexi and I were partway through a four-hour drive to the lovely seaside town of Cape May, New Jersey. I had no plan to wonder on the way—it was to be a straight shot to the destination. But the joy of heading out to the beach with a friend for several days of writing and relaxation had me feeling slightly giddy. As the sun set behind us, we cruised around downtown Philadelphia and crossed the Delaware River into New Jersey, heading for a quick stop at Starbucks for refueling. In my experience this is rarely a bad idea.

Chai latte now in cupholder, I merged back onto the highway into the growing darkness, paying attention only to my GPS. Several moments later, I came upon a massive bridge with the twinkling lights of a fairly large city on the other side. I immediately felt that bizarre feeling of excitement that explorers know well. What was this place? It was unexpected and a little disorienting as I didn't realize I would encounter another city on my way to the shore. About halfway across the bridge, craning to see signs or other tell-tale indications that would enlighten me, I noticed a sign for the Benjamin Franklin Bridge. Funny, since one would think a name like that would more likely relate to Philadelphia than driving east toward the ocean. Except I was. Heading into Philadelphia. Again.

Bad enough that I blindly followed my GPS, completely not noticing that it was taking me back home. But to drive on the very same road that I had just come from, across the very same bridge into the VERY SAME CITY, all the while thinking I was somewhere entirely new. Dumb. But kind of hilarious. I still laugh at myself when I think of it.

A word of advice: Don't trade in your brain for your GPS!

> **Additional navigation tips, resources, and information can be found at: www.wonderbingtravel.com/book-resources**

Chapter 14

Lodging

The Lord replied, "My Presence will go with you,
and I will give you rest."

Exodus 33:14

Road-tripping will wear you out. It's a fact. At the end of most days, I am happy-tired and almost always excited to settle down for the evening, no matter where I plan to lay my weary head. I've learned there is wisdom in knowing when to stop, relax, and reset. Whenever possible, I do my best to build wonder into where I stay. It doesn't all happen on the road!

No matter how many times I swing open the door to a hotel room or pull up to an Airbnb or campsite, there's forever a tiny thrill of discovery. My heart beats just a little faster—a mini bit of wonder. These initial moments often confirm that my advance research (or my gut feeling) paid off. When I experience occasional disappointments, I salvage what I can and learn from it for the next time. Chances are there's a lesson and a good story!

Making great decisions about where to stay at night does more than provide delight to the end of the day. It allows space for much needed rest and recovery. I'm always amazed at how tired I can be from simply driving. In *Travels with Charley in Search of America*, John Steinbeck reflected on this phenomenon:

"Consider then the small, unnoticed turning of the steering wheel, . . . the varying pressure of foot on accelerator . . . then there are the muscles of shoulders and neck, constantly if unconsciously flexed for emergency, the eyes darting from road to rear-view mirror, the thousand decisions so deep that the conscious mind is not aware of them. The output of energy, nervous and muscular, is enormous."[1]

All this before we step out of the car and really *do* anything! Your days will be full, you will be tired, and it's important that your nights provide rest.

Keep in mind that decisions regarding your lodging will connect and overlap with other essentials we've already explored. Time and distance, budget, and navigation all play significant roles. As we dive deeper into the fun of planning your lodging, you'll naturally begin to pivot toward fitting it all together in a way that suits your style and sense of adventuring.

The topic of lodging provides a real risk for information overload. With that in mind, the chapter itself will focus on accommodation options and exploring significant deciding factors as you consider which choices work best for your particular adventure. We'll end with helpful examples of both pre-planned and spontaneous lodging for short and longer trips.

Types of Lodging

When I first began solo road-tripping, I was on a seriously tight budget. I slept in the back of my SUV at times, stayed with friends, and occasionally treated myself to a night at an Airbnb or a hotel. While I'm still always working within my budget, I now save in advance so my days on the road are not quite so squeaky tight. My biggest money saver? I've fallen in love with camping (more about my super cool set-up in the resources). My first-time camping preparations felt a bit overwhelming at the outset, but I was determined and looked at it as an adventure within the adventure! Once I learned the basics, camping became my hands-down favorite lodging option.

I've also learned there are plenty of ingenious and creative accommodation options out there if you know where to look. I will provide you with a list of options here, and you'll find the chapter resources drill down into details and additional pros and cons of each, including links and reservation information.

Solo Road-Trip Lodging Options:
- Motel/Motor lodges
- Airbnb
- Vrbo
- Camping

- Hipcamp
- Bed and Breakfasts
- Big Box Stores parking lots
- Cracker Barrel parking Lots
- Fitness Center parking lots
- Truck stops
- Friends and Family

So you're likely scratching your head over a few of these options. Parking lots? Hipcamp? These are all viable options! You get to choose what makes you comfortable, both mentally and physically! The chapter resources share all the details, but here are a few thoughts on the outliers so you know what's what:

Hipcamp

Hands down, Hipcamp has become one of my favorite road-tripping lodging options. The concept is similar to Airbnb but is designed for campers. The website is great, there's an app for your phone, and, like Airbnb, individuals advertise different lodging options for you to view and book. According to their site, "Hipcamp has grown into the most comprehensive resource for discovering and booking unique outdoor stays including tent camping, RV parks, cabins, treehouses, and glamping." The price can be completely free or quite expensive, but most range in the less-than-$50-per-night category.

I have used Hipcamp to book some fantastic camping options, including a truly cool out-of-the-way campground on top of a mountain in Colorado (free), a small family-run ranch in eastern Wyoming ($25), and even a gorgeous farm in Wisconsin ($35) complete with alpacas and disc golf courses. Every experience has been stellar so far! Each listing also provides details regarding access to showers and other amenities. As mentioned, some Hipcamp hosts offer cabins and glamping options, so you don't have to have an RV or tent to make the most of it!

Parking Lots

Yes, parking lots. While not for everyone, there are some significant upsides to sleeping in your vehicle. Let's start with the free part! No overnight parking lot option I am aware of charges their guests one penny. Larger stores such as Walmart, Sam's Club, Costco and Home Depot all allow overnight parking, in addition to Cracker Barrel, truck stops and fitness centers. In all cases, it's best to check with the individual store to ensure there aren't any local laws prohibiting car camping.

If you drive an SUV, truck, or van, overnight "car camping" can be a satisfying way to spend the night. There are plenty of ingenious ways to create sleeping spaces in your vehicle that go far beyond the recline button on the front seat! If you're interested in details, check out the end-of-chapter resources.

While big truck stops (think Love's or Flying J-type mega stops) offer overnight options, I would only use them as a last resort for sleeping. I just don't think I would feel comfortable there alone, not to mention the constant noise. However, they do offer fairly remarkable shower amenities for a small fee. For about $12, you have access to upscale hotel-quality private bathrooms with vanities, toilets and showers. Both companies mentioned above have apps to reserve in advance, ensuring your shower is waiting for you when you arrive!

Several nationwide fitness clubs also offer overnight parking. If you're a member, then you can take full advantage of the showers and restrooms too. If you happen to be a Planet Fitness Black Card member, the hydromassage and deep tissue chairs are a wonderful benefit to massage a weary body!

Each type of location may provide a list of restrictions, but, in a nutshell, car camping in a parking lot means that you stay in your car. No outdoor "tailgate-style" eating, no fires, no noise, etc. Parking areas are usually well-lit and well-maintained. Always check the website or call with questions.

Motor Lodges

Back in the middle of the 20th century, traveling the new interstates across the US often involved spending a night or two in a motor lodge. You can call them motels, too, but you'll likely have a more accurate picture in your head when you think of a "motor lodge." So many of these once hip and trendy motels are now falling down and worn out, super sketchy, or just plain gone from this earth, but an increasing number have been rescued and rejuvenated into something special. I've stayed in a few—one in Bend, Oregon, and another in the Adirondacks—and both were very cool experiences that provided their own wonder. A little Google or Instagram research will reveal dozens of fun and funky options from California to Maine.

Deciding Factors

When I daydream about a road trip, my imagination often leads me to visions of unique and charming overnight bungalows and cabins, or a campsite on a lake watching the moon rise and the stars shine above the fire. There's something about making a very temporary home in another place that fuels my sense of adventure. I bring those daydreams into my reality when I plan, but there are almost always some key factors to consider. Some of these decisions are made before I leave, but longer trips generally lead to some last-moment or at least day-of choices as well. It's all adventure!

Before you start making decisions, let's weigh a few particulars that can be the difference between embarking on a clear path to wonder and rest, or creating a potential mess. You may come up with additional considerations that are unique to you as well.

Budget

Sigh. It always comes back to the money, doesn't it? Let's embrace that idea though, because keeping it front of mind typically leads to smart choices you won't regret later! Sticking to your budget doesn't mean sucking the fun out of your trip. It means you'll be able to immerse yourself more fully in each day because you'll have a sense both of where you'll end your days and how much it may cost.

Remember that on most road trips, lodging and gas will be your most costly expenditures. Deciding where to stay at night is intrinsically connected to your budget, and that connection will play a significant role in your planning. Put a dollar amount on your lodging as part of your budget planning. You may not have everything exactly laid out before you leave, but now that you've been exposed to a long list of possibilities, you can do a little research and create a fairly accurate estimate.

Planning vs. Spontaneity

It can be tricky to decide when to make reservations in advance, thus pinning yourself down to a specific end point for the day, and when to just figure it out as you go. The choice is driven primarily by your priorities.

Consider what is important to you. How valuable is peace of mind and confidence gained by knowing where you'll end the day? Maybe you prefer having the freedom to drive for as long as the mood strikes you? It's possible both approaches will appeal at different times within the same trip. The trick is to find a balance that works for you.

It's relatively simple to plan specific nightly destinations for a long weekend, but on lengthier trips, that approach can quickly become overwhelming instead of comforting. When I'm traveling more than a few consecutive days, I often give myself more freedom to figure things out as I go. That doesn't mean I have zero idea where I may end up on a given day. While that scenario may occasionally occur, it's more likely that I've checked my general route and know within reason how far I may go. Most often I'll do enough research to know what my options in that area might be. Are there reasonably priced hotels/motels? Nice campgrounds or state parks? Plenty of Airbnbs? Before I ever leave home, I typically do enough research to have a sense of each area, but if I'm figuring it out en route, I often spend a little time online early in the day, investigating the possibilities for the upcoming evening.

Once again, there's no blueprint for managing this. You

may find comfort in having a solid confirmation number in hand for each night of the trip. Or you may find, like some, that being bound by deadlines or reservations creates stress. If you're just not sure what will work for you initially, make the choice that provides the most confidence! I promise you will make both wise and poor decisions in this area. It's all part of your story and it will work out.

The Middle of Nothing

There may be some legs of a road adventure that land you squarely in the middle of nothing at the end of a day, which I do not recommend! In many states, this is unlikely, but there are pockets of wilderness all across our country, and if you're off-highway exploring, it can be a little intimidating to find yourself without options when you're tired and ready to end the day.

To alleviate this unenviable possibility, be sure to generally scope out your route for the day before you begin the morning. If you're heading into desolate territory, have a basic plan and preferably a backup plan as well. Often my backup involves driving further than I originally hoped, but if it leads to a safe and comfortable end to a long day, I'm all for it.

Traveling with Your Dog

Road-tripping with your pooch will limit your options, especially if you're trying to find last-minute lodgings. Happily, I can share from personal experience that the positives far outweigh the negatives. Because I travel so often with Lexi the Golden and hate going without her, I've devoted an entire chapter to the ins and outs of traveling with a furry friend.

There are plenty of pros, some definite downsides, and we'll explore them all in that chapter.

Safety

I love seeking wonder on a solo road trip, and ideally, we all should be able to explore anywhere without fear. It would be foolish, however, to travel with rose-colored glasses. Not every situation or every person is free of evil or malicious intent, and while highly unlikely, it is possible for you to find yourself in less than desirable circumstances.

We will devote an entire chapter to thinking through best practices to set yourself up for an adventure filled with peace and security. It's hard to seek freedom and wonder if much of your time is consumed with worry, so we'll take time to properly delve into all it.

Safety regarding your choice of lodging is truly a personal choice. For example, I feel completely safe camping in a tent by myself (or with Lexi). I typically seek out state parks, in part because they tend to check everyone at entry, the restroom facilities are lit at night, and there are other campers close by (but not too close!). Some women may not feel comfortable in that situation. No problem! Do what works for you. If that means hotel stays only, then knowing that about yourself enables you to plan accordingly.

Consider each scenario that you may encounter. Would you feel comfortable sleeping in the back of your vehicle in a lighted parking lot? What about at a motel where the door to your room has outside access? When the answer is a flat-out "no," then don't do it! For those places that do appeal but may still bring safety concerns, check them out thoroughly in advance. Look at each website carefully and make direct contact with the owner/proprietor before you commit.

While you can't predict every safety factor, doing your homework will go a long way toward ensuring your stay adds wonder to your trip, rather than fear or anxiety.

How It Really Works

Feeling a little overwhelmed? Endless possibilities can have that effect, but options are a glorious thing! I know we can all get stuck in the muck of the sheer number of choices and ideas, but one of the great joys of a road trip is designing our personal path to wonder in a way that speaks to our unique passions.

As you consider what types of accommodations appeal and how to make those work in your pursuit of wonder, allow me to share a few illustrations of how I've managed on different occasions: first, a short trip (3 nights), followed by a longer one from which I've extracted two weeks—one fairly planned out and another done on a wing and a prayer. There are no checklists here, just examples, a little reflection on what worked and what didn't, and hopefully a bit of inspiration!

Short Trip

For the past several years, I have planned short road trips for my parents where I act as travel planner and guide. We have a grand time, and they get to continue to explore a bit of the world without dealing with the details. Other than some advance budget discussions, their only jobs are to pack their own stuff, get in the car, and bring snacks. While traveling with my parents creates an entirely different vibe than pursuing wonder on my own, it provides a great illustration for planning lodging on a short trip.

A recent adventure led us into upstate New York for three nights and four days. Our main destination was Adirondack Park, which covers six million acres of both public and private land. In other words, it's enormous. I did a fair amount of research to learn more, and as our time was somewhat limited, I navigated a route that focused on the days and nights in and around the park and not on the drive up and back.

After fairly evenly dividing our travel distance and time for each day, I began to search for cool places to stay. For this adventure, lodging would play a large role in the wonder of the trip, and I was determined to book three unique and memorable stays. In the end, we enjoyed a magnificent night in a beautiful old lodge, landed an extremely cool and eclectic stay in a newly remodeled vintage motor inn at the foot of Whiteface Mountain, and spoiled ourselves in the charm and beauty of the restored Queensbury Hotel in Glens Falls. Each wildly different yet perfect for this particular trip.

Our reserved lodgings were strung together by entire days that included very little planning. We stopped and started whenever we wished with no agenda other than to finish our day where our accommodations were reserved. The "golden hours" were chock full of the unexpected, and we stumbled into wonder over and over again. Could we have left home with no reservations? For sure, but in this case making advance plans was a priority for a few reasons:

- I was not traveling alone and needed to ensure the comfort of my parents.

- The park is vast, and some areas are sparsely populated, so advance research for an end point to each day was crucial.

- It was early summer and close to prime vacation time

for many folks. I didn't want to struggle to find lodgings at the last minute only to find "No Vacancy" signs everywhere.

- The trip was relatively short, so plotting end points for each day didn't require guesswork.

- Our lodging was an intentional part of the wonder of this trip.

Long Road Trip

Planning every night of a long road trip would be a struggle for me. I thrive with a "flexible schedule," and, for me, all that advance planning adds way too much pressure to sustain day after day. It leaves no room for a spontaneous decision to change routes, skip a location, or stay longer when I happen upon something magical.

However, when I'm plotting and planning lengthier trips, I almost always make reservations for the first few nights. I map out how far I plan to drive those initial days, and reserve accordingly. As I'm typically traveling thousands of miles overall, starting off with a few certainties gives me confidence, and it's likely I've obsessed a bit over those first days anyway! Further into the trip I tend to feel more sure in my wanderings, so I often pivot to a more impulsive plan that I can adjust on a daily basis, always keeping in mind my rough goal for the miles and time I want to cover each day.

Many factors influence my decisions about how far to travel on any given day, and every trip tells a story all its own. Most of my road trips break down fairly evenly between the nights I plan and the ones I figure out as I go.

A Planned Week—Central PA to Sheridan, WY

I love planning the first hitch of a long road trip. I fully embrace the feeling of endless possibility. On this particular adventure I labored in love over those first six nights quite a bit before I ever left home. It involved a lot of plotting and I enjoyed most every minute. My choice! On the road, each day unfolded easily, with only a few smallish issues. Knowing each morning where I planned to end the day gave me confidence to strike out and seek wonder with my eyes wide open.

I had created a route that would take Lexi the Golden and me west into Ohio and then north into Michigan's Upper Peninsula before heading west through Wisconsin, Minnesota, and North Dakota. Since much of the territory we would cover comprised farmland, forest, and small cities, it made sense to seek out campgrounds, Airbnbs, and the occasional chain hotel.

Our first day of adventure began and ended on the highway, our night spent in a hotel. When I'm traveling across many states, I often use that initial day to make time toward our first real destination. In this case, Lexi and I landed for the evening in Bay City, Michigan, and a good night's sleep set us up for subsequent days of camping along the Great Lakes. I love to camp, and I love it more if I can sleep in a lovely bed and take a wonderful shower after a few days of roughing it! So, on Day Four we arrived just across the North Dakota border in Grand Forks, ready to relax comfortably for an evening.

North Dakota proved to be charming in every way, and not what I expected at all! Incredibly lush and green, the rich landscape was dotted with lakes and beribboned by the wide, blue Missouri River. I daydreamed about Lewis and Clark and anticipated discovery around every bend. We traversed most of the state on Day Five before stopping to camp at an outstanding state park named for those intrepid explorers. Settled in by late evening, we enjoyed a fiery sunset as the moon rose up over the lake-wide Missouri to assume its nightly vigil.

When I was scheming to find an interesting spot for our last night's lodging before we landed at our destination in Wyoming, I kept coming up empty. In western North Dakota there are very few towns, which equates to meager lodging options of any kind. I finally found a cute little house on Airbnb located in the mid-sized town of Dickinson, and it served Lexi and me well. After a great sleep I drove the final leg to Sheridan, Wyoming, arriving rested and ready for mountain adventures with friends!

Spontaneity – Sheridan, WY to Westcliffe, CO

This may be my favorite way to explore, though that wasn't always the case. I have earned my carefree confidence over the course of many thousands of miles and now years of experience winging it. I don't love starting a road trip this way, but once I'm in deep, it's fun to wander, and inevitably I encounter more wonder.

I had one week to make this drive, which in reality could be done in a single day if necessary. I loved knowing I had seven days to meander through Wyoming and Colorado, transforming the direct shot of 560 miles into 1,560. I did, however, plan a few "anchors" into the week to give me some touchpoints. Establishing an anchor of sorts into most days fulfills my need for some kind of order. That anchor can be a hike, a town, a lake, or waterfall. It could be a visit with a friend, indulgence at a restaurant, or a stop at a national park. It can also be a reservation for wherever I plan to spend the night. Whatever it is, it serves as the known part of my day and frees me to see where the Spirit leads me for the rest.

The anchors I built into this week included reservations at two campgrounds: one night in Grand Teton National Park near Jackson, Wyoming, and another north of Steamboat Springs in Colorado. Especially in national parks like Grand Teton, you must reserve months in advance if you want a good spot. I also planned to visit Rocky Mountain National Park in Colorado, though I had no plan to find lodging in or near the park.

The unplanned hours fulfilled my wondering urge to stop and start and turn wherever the road called. I was unconcerned about finding places to stay. The path from northeastern Wyoming to southern Colorado boasts innumerable small towns, state and national parks, private campgrounds, and "Mom and Pop" motels, not to mention interstate highways with plenty of chain hotels that would work in a pinch. All that meant I could confidently wander until day's end.

Okay, that sounds idyllic, and mostly it was! Lexi and I did encounter two occasions where lack of planning created extra driving in one case, and a little stress in another. In both cases, things worked out perfectly, but know that a feature of winging it is that there isn't always a perfect option when you want one. These are always great moments to pray for clarity, wisdom, and common sense to rule the day.

At week's end, we had camped in three state parks and one national park, splurged for an evening in a cabin on a ranch, and enjoyed one hotel room as a last resort and another because I needed a break. That July week remains one of my favorite travel times ever. There was a wildness to it, with just enough of a plan woven through to keep me anchored and confident.

These are my stories, but endless possibilities stretch out before you! As you navigate the options, take time to pray for God to grant you the wisdom to make confident and thoughtful choices. My prayer for each of you throughout this journey is that He will lead you to what He wants you to see and experience as you seek His glory in all the wonder He created for us to delight in. Enjoy the planning, and take time to examine all the additional resources to help you gain insight and confidence as you seek out wonder-filled places to lay your weary adventurous head!

**Additional lodging tips, resources,
and information can be found at:
www.wonderbingtravel.com/book-resources**

Chapter 15

Food/Drink

It doesn't matter how old you are. Buying snacks for a road trip should always look like an unsupervised 9-year-old was given $100.

—Unknown

This quote makes me want to run out and buy all the things, pack my bags, and hit the road. I find great joy and perhaps a misdirected sense of fulfillment in shopping for road-trip goodies. It's not unlike another great love—school supply shopping. Both are infused with a sense of anticipation, fresh starts, and possibility. I can trace back my emotional connection for "goodie" shopping to the generosity of my grandmother. She spoiled my sister and me incessantly, often handing each of us a quarter and sending us into the local five and dime to gleefully fill our paper bags with Bit-O-Honeys,

B-B-Bats, and Bazooka Bubble Gum. Yes, I am a child of the 70s!

For me, buying snacks in anticipation of a road trip reigns as one of the most exciting parts of road-trip prepping. Of course, being on the road, whether for a weekend or a month, requires more than piles of sugar and feel-good snacks. There are wonderful meals and experiences to relish as you traverse our beautiful country. You can plan for it or you can wing it, and chances are you'll do a bit of both.

And so we arrive at our last pillar of planning. As with lodging, it would be easy to become tangled in the many weeds of endless choice. I'll reserve the details for the end-of-chapter resources and stick to the high ground here.

More Than Fuel

Few things in our lives are more personal than food. Our choices regarding when, where, how, and what we eat each day are as unique to each of us as our DNA. Anthony Bourdain put it this way: "Food is everything we are. It's an extension of nationalist feeling, ethnic feeling, your personal history, your province, your region, your tribe, your grandma. It's inseparable from those from the get-go."

We cannot separate who we are from our love of what we eat! As we think about food on a road trip, let's keep this concept in mind for multiple reasons. First, your adventure is made both unique and fascinating by your eating choices. Your comfort food may not be my comfort food. You may prefer to skip breakfast and enjoy a large lunch, or simply snack through the day and anticipate a soul-satisfying supper. And it's not just the order and amount of what we eat! Our individual health, palates, desire for grease versus vegetables, caffeine at day's dawn or sparkling lemon water—all are particularly personal and sometimes peculiar! You, happily, make all those choices as you blissfully fill your own belly.

Bourdain's quote is also an encouragement to adopt an attitude of open-minded curiosity, inviting an education for the taste buds. You will encounter endless opportunities to learn about the culinary culture of the places you pass through. America is huge, and each state and regional area boasts incredible and unusual delicacies and tastes. Often these are based on the ethnic heritage in the region, but in some cases, a region's pride in their claim to, say, "best cheesesteak" or "best barbecue" has evolved in more recent history.

Food is a pretty good prism through which to view humanity.

—Jonathan Gold

Wherever you find food there will be people there to eat it. Mealtime inherently connects us to others. Eating out when we travel, even if alone, provides connection to other souls, including diners, wait staff, hosts, and cashiers. Some days it may be the greatest amount of time you spend in the company of others. Make the most of it! James Beard, famous chef from the early days of television, quipped, "Food is our common ground, a universal experience."

I have found that, despite my reservations about eating alone, the situation creates easy opportunities to find connection with others, which often leads to great conversation. Settling down at a counter or table for a leisurely lunch or dinner has opened the door to many insightful and enriching exchanges with both locals and other travelers. And for those times you choose to enjoy your meal quietly, you are free to fully indulge in people-watching!

The decisions you'll make about food will lead to their own magic as you wander. Keep in mind, wonder is just as easily revealed in the splendor of a food truck or an old diner as in the jaw-stopping glories of the natural beauty around us. Don't miss either one! Pull over often, try the local coffee, savor the homemade ice cream, eat the fresh berries, deep-fried comfort food, or world's best barbecue, and let all the joys of sight and smell and taste weave their way into your adventure.

For Those Who Plan

Sometimes the greatest meals on vacations are the ones you find when Plan A falls through."

—Anthony Bourdain

As romantically adventurous as all of this may sound, a bit of planning will ease your way toward the world's greatest French fries or fresh-pressed honey lavender iced tea. In addition to the essentials of planning, time and experience will lead you to what works best for your unique tastes and situations. That's code for it probably won't be just as you imagined, but I'll wager it'll be just right. Whatever plan you devise regarding food, hold it loosely. With rare exceptions, it's not too difficult to create or stumble into a satisfying Plan B!

The advantages to outlining a plan for your food needs (and cravings) increase relative to the length of your trip. If you're planning a weekend away, managing how and where and what you'll eat doesn't require the same attention as does figuring out how to navigate your meals for weeks on the road.

> **Tip:** *If you're camping and making your own meals, even for a portion of your trip, you'll need to plan more deliberately. Information and checklists for campers are included in the resource section to ensure you have everything you need!*

Inevitably, most food-related planning relates to personal choice and your individual daily routine. What follows here is literally food for thought, including insight into planning based on my own routines and preferences. Make the choices that appeal to you!

We can't get away from considering budget here. Your decisions about road-trip food can make a significant impact on your wallet. Where you eat will affect considerably how much money you spend. If you're planning a more extensive adventure, you're more likely to need some cost-effective options for eating. As we all know, eating out every day depletes the bank account before you can say "venti vanilla latte, please!"

Let's dig into food planning for both short and longer travel.

The Short Journey

The more condensed the adventure, the more I focus on enjoying local food at least once each day. I don't want to miss out on anything! While I never go any distance without a serious stash of snacks, my meals on a shorter journey, as well as my indulgences, tend to be purchased and enjoyed wherever my SUV leads me.

In the previous chapter I shared the lodging scheme for my Adirondack adventure. That journey also lends itself well to this discussion. You may recall I had secured all our lodging in advance, but none of the eating. My mom presided over the snacks (where do you think I learned this stuff?), I sought out great places to eat, and my dad was charged with enjoying whatever he ordered. We were all aptly suited to the jobs at hand.

Over the course of three days, here's how it worked out:

Day 1 – After an early breakfast at my parent's Central PA home, we headed north to Ithaca, New York, to spend a few hours enjoying lunch at a local pub with my college roommate. By dinnertime we had arrived at our quaint little lodge near Eagle Bay, New York, where we savored both the local cuisine and an otherworldly sunset from the lodge dining room.

Day 2 – We enjoyed a hearty breakfast at the lodge before heading further into the northern woods, stopping here and there to see the sights, shop, and eat. The very first town on our trek boasted some pretty wonderful lattes, which improved my happy disposition even further. As homemade ice cream abounds in that area, we indulged on at least one occasion that afternoon, and ate our share of munchies in the car. Before settling down in our vintage motor lodge for the night, we dove into summer comfort food at a local bar and grille, recommended to us by the lodge's hostess. Asking the locals for their personal favorites rarely leads to disappointment! Looking back, this day's fare was not exactly a model of healthy food choices, though I am sure we had veggies and fruit in the car!

Day 3 – I ignored breakfast that morning to chase waterfalls on the mountain, though my parents enjoyed the continental version provided by the motel. We made up for our lack of serious sustenance with a stop at the local chocolate factory to sample all the goodies, but sadly there was no coffee shop in the area. We drove throughout the afternoon, pausing long enough for a late "lunch" of more homemade ice cream and car snacks, and we capped off the last evening of our trip with a fantastic meal at an Italian restaurant in downtown Glens Falls.

Our first night's dinner at the lodge was our only planned meal; I had called ahead to ensure the dining room would be open. While the territory we covered those few days included vast forested areas, small towns and hamlets abounded, so we were never far from possibility. We chose what "looked good," which of course is an undefinable and quite unscientific method, to ensure we found the local hotspots. We asked for dinner recommendations our second evening, and when we arrived in Glens Falls, I did a bit of scouting and online research before settling on our quaint Italian restaurant.

I love knowing that no one else could have possibly made these identical choices while driving the same three-day route. We were quite content with ours, and they served our needs and exceeded our expectations at every turn.

Long Trip

I learned a long time ago that trying to micromanage the perfect vacation is always a disaster. That leads to terrible times.

—Anthony Bourdain

Micromanaging any part of a road trip saps our opportunities to wonder, to invite God into our days and ask Him to show us His glory in His creation. It's fair to say this applies to food too! On a longer road trip, look to find the balance between what you can do to prep and plan in advance and what can be left unplanned. Preparation provides a base of what's needed so that your time on the road can be focused on the treasures in front of you. Open space in your planning leaves room for you to stumble upon the unexpected and seek out those special places hidden around the bend in your new terrain. It will take some trial and error the first few times, but you'll find your sweet spot!

Do consider your budget, the length of your trip, and your own proclivities toward eating. One of the simple joys of solo road-tripping is eating when, where, and what you want! Keep in mind that more planning typically leads to less spending. Finding a happy balance leads to a more soul-satisfying trip. Even if your budget can take a huge hit on food, there's wisdom in packing a cooler and a bag of goodies to ensure, no matter where you are, you'll never be hangry!

Over the years I've honed my approach to food for weeks-long travel. Before I share my basic strategy, you should know how food and I work together. I do my best to eat healthy without becoming consumed by it. A road trip means treating myself now and then, whether that involves buying chocolate-covered cashews for the car or stopping for custard in Wisconsin. I typically drink my breakfast (caffeine, please!) and add a little fruit, snack a bit in the car, pull over somewhere to create lunch from my stash in my cooler, snack a bit again during the afternoon, and then settle down for dinner. Sometimes dinner comes out of the cooler, but often I seek out a local meal. Camping comprises 30–40% of my trips, so I do some meal prep and cooking in advance to make dinners at the campsites easy.

But . . . any of that can change multiple times on any given day. The fun oxymoron in all of this is that planning frees me to be spontaneous whenever the mood strikes me. I always have options with me but can pivot to a more fun or satisfying choice when one surfaces. It could very well be a Chick-fil-A sign that alters my plans, a food truck offering up fish tacos, or a diner advertising homemade waffles. And of course, ice cream. I never know!

The other distinguishing factor in my personal planning is Lexi the Golden. While some restaurants have dog-friendly patios or other outdoor seating, many do not. If I choose to eat out, there are times when take-out is the only option. Depending on my lodging for the night, I may be able to leave her home to snooze, but most often she is with me, curled up under a patio table with a bowl of water and plenty of pats on the head from other patrons. The upcoming chapter on road-tripping with your dog will dive deeper into all of this!

Here's how I generally map out food for a trip of a week or more:

Snacks: Lots of fruit and raw veggies. I typically take my long trips in the summer, so there are plenty of fresh options. I buy my favorite yummy things, including kettle corn and a homemade trail mix with plenty of chocolate and nuts. Beef jerky, protein bars, pretzels, and dried fruit all find their way into my goodie bag as well. I keep a small cooler up front for chilled snacks and a zippered reusable grocery bag for the rest.

Breakfast: If I do choose to eat breakfast, it's usually a bar and some fruit to go along with my caffeine fix. It's also difficult for me to drive by a local bakery without stopping. Sampling sticky buns and cinnamon rolls is a valid research endeavor!

Lunch: I just never know how this is going to go. As the lunch hour is smack in the middle of my wanderings, I rarely know what I'll encounter. It may be as simple as a quick picnic to break up the day or lunch while I'm driving, but often I'm eating food I have with me. I have several go-to favorites that travel well. These are made a day or two before I leave home and make for easy eating on the road. Alternatively, if I pass something enticing, I may opt to stop instead.

Dinner: My budget and I have several conversations about this because it's very easy for me to choose fun food out over the less expensive alternatives I have packed. If I'm eating out, I keep it local and look for dog-friendly outdoor seating and great places to people-watch. On nights without Lexi, I try to find places where eating at a bar or counter looks inviting, or I seek out little restaurants in the heart of a small town where I might make conversation with the locals.

A peculiarity about food and a road trip—I tend to be hungry at odd times, snack when I'm driving, but generally eat less overall. Did I mention snacking? I love all the goodies!

Check out the end-of-chapter resources for my shopping lists, specific food ideas, and recipes for some of my favorite travel dishes. In the upcoming Packing chapter's resources, I'll share my favorite coolers and containers for storing food for the road.

Tips

Mistakes will be made. I've made plenty—spending more than I planned, purchasing and making ahead enough food for four people instead of one, and driving miles off my route to stop at a now boarded-up, out-of-business restaurant. On the bright side, here are a few things I've learned along the way.

Healthy Eating

The hours we spend merely perched on our bottoms while driving rank high as an unavoidable drawback to being on the road. While our brains are busy navigating and soaking in the wonder, our bodies aren't enjoying the same level of joy. Stiff joints, a sore back, and achy legs are part of the package, especially if you're not in your 20s anymore! All that sitting can also mess with your digestion.

Lots of stretching, drinking plenty of water, and stopping often certainly help, but quality snacking and meals can offer a boost as well. Packing healthy snacks that are good for your gut will keep you energized and alert. Berries, apples, bananas, and nuts are all great pick-me-ups! I do love my sugar, but I try not to overindulge as it often leads to a mid-afternoon slump.

Eating out is a fun part of your adventure too. You should absolutely enjoy trying new and local foods! Not every meal you order out will be healthy, so opt for a side of veggies when you can and drink lots of water with your meals.

Snack Sizes

I've found the best way not to overindulge with snack foods is to take the time to portion them out before I leave home.

Even the healthiest of fruits are better eaten in moderation! Of course, there are also chips and pretzels within arm's reach at all times, but everything that can be portioned out is divided into individual sandwich or snack bags so I only eat what's in the bag. Side benefits: it's easy to grab what I want without stopping and the little bags minimize crumbs and spillage.

Farmer's Markets

We all love our hometown farmer's market, so why not seek out new ones on your travels? Both large and small towns usually have a market at least one day each week. A quick online search will reveal those closest to you, usually with days and times. Many markets offer significantly more than fresh produce. Great local coffee and other beverages, fresh meats, cheese, and bakery items are all likely to be on hand. Frequently, local restaurants and food trucks also set up shop at markets with plenty of ready-to-eat meals. The vibe can be festive as well, with many markets hosting live music, arts and crafts vendors, yummy desserts, and even dog-friendly treat stalls.

The local market acts as a microcosm of its surrounding community, where you can learn about the area by observing the myriad stalls that showcase all kinds of businesses, people, and food. Within minutes you'll know if the vibe is friendly or standoffish, casual or stuffy. You'll know what is important to that particular town—are they into coffee or kombucha? Pulled pork or acai bowls? Stock up on produce, try something new and fun, and sit back to people-watch for a bit.

Bakeries

So, okay, "eating healthy" and "bakeries" don't intuitively

fit well together, but you're a big girl and can make your own decisions. I call it research! Another go-to when visiting a new town is the local downtown bakery. Follow your nose, especially in the mornings. Specific baked goods can be quite regional, so depending where your travels take you, you may encounter funnel cakes and warm homemade doughnuts, croissants and scones, or sticky buns and cinnamon rolls. I advise sampling a bit wherever you go!

Be Flexible

I'm all for doing some food planning and creating a few expectations for my trips, but I also try to hold it all very loosely. Don't forget to embrace what's in front of you. Try new things and keep your eyes open to unusual opportunities. On the flip side, keep enough food with you to get you through any unexpected situations where you need to shift your original plan for the day.

Take Care of You

Some of us are better at self-care than others, but paying attention to your day-to-day needs when you are road-tripping by yourself should be a non-negotiable part of each day. This sentiment echoes back to Chapter 8's Personal Peace, where you took inventory of your daily heart and head needs. An important part of creating a framework you can thrive in absolutely involves what you eat and drink each day. Without ensuring that you restore yourself daily, your pursuit of wonder will flounder.

The Long Trip Refresh

I love starting a road trip fully fortified with snacks, drink, and a cooler (or two) full of favorites. Everything works like a dream for the first five days or so, and I pat myself on the back for my girl scout level of preparedness. But wait! On day six the salsa is almost gone, the veggies are getting mushy, and no amount of refrigeration is going to save that barbecue chicken or salami. Ugh. I rely on several homemade dishes to sustain me for that first week on the road. But cooler food has a shelf life if I haven't already eaten it. Now what?

I tend to pause mid-trip to do some cooler cleaning and grocery shopping for fruits, veggies, and meal items. It's easy to forego this and eat out from that point on, but what happens when no lunch or dinner options are available? Not to mention the added expense. Pretzels and granola bars will eventually leave you cranky and your body needs real food.

I try to seek out stores with plenty of pre-made meal options and great produce. Many large grocery stores have make-to-order delis, main dishes like fried chicken and sides, plenty of premade salads and soups, even sushi bars. I stock up on items that will last for 3-4 days, can be eaten cold if necessary, and then get back on the road.

Keeping It Cool

The longer your trip, the more often you'll need to replenish your ice or refreeze your cooler inserts. This is one reason I opt for a hotel or Airbnb every 3rd or 4th day. Most rooms have refrigerators and freezers, so I haul my cooler into the room and pop the contents into the fridge until I leave. Everything is kept cool, and I can start anew with ice. If the freezer is large enough, I refreeze my cooler inserts and they are good to go for another three days. While I haven't tried this option personally, a friend shared that some hotels have freezer space you can borrow during your stay!

One other perk of the hotel room is the microwave. Most

food I travel with can be eaten cold, but it's nice to warm things up occasionally.

Time for a Toast

Our relationships with food can be so complicated. Planning meals for a weeks-long road trip—also complicated. But what about drinking? Thankfully, this is so much easier. While our choices for food and drink often go hand-in-hand, a discussion solely about what you'll drink on your adventure involves far less thinking than all our talk of food.

And while less complicated, my unscientific opinion is that women typically have strong relationships with our beverages of choice. I most definitely do. In fact, I feel quite resolute about beginning every day possible with a chai latte. They make me happy, warm, and are connected to feelings of contentment. Most women I know have proprietary feelings that lean toward obsession about their beverages. Coffee or tea, kombucha, smoothies, fizzy water or still, sweet tea or absolutely-only unsweet tea, beer or wine (and then the obvious next question – red or white?). We all have opinions. Wars could be waged on the topic.

Whatever your penchant is, include it in your planning. Consider what you love and need and keep it as simple as possible. If that means packing only water and buying cold drinks as you go, do it! Keep in mind that drinks take up lots of space, so packing a case of water or Gatorades might not work for your vehicle.

I'm a three-drink road-tripper: chai lattes, water, and the occasional glass of wine. I'm in favor of trying new things as I go, but these provide joy and satisfy basic needs.

- Most mornings I seek out a local coffee shop to take care of the latte "issue," though to give credence to my level of dependence on my little vice, I confess that I also travel with cartons of liquid chai, milk, and a small frother I can plug in to make my own.

- I always keep a few gallons of water in the car and a 32-ounce refillable water bottle up front with me. I try to drink two full bottles a day. Hydration is not something to mess with on a road trip, and if you're traveling in the dry west or southwest, drink plenty, and then drink some more.

- I usually leave home with a bottle or two of wine. Enjoying a glass of wine some evenings not only helps me settle down and rest but adds to my celebratory reflections at the end of the day.

Cups of Joy

Take the drinks you love along for the ride but keep your eyes open for wonderful opportunities to stop and sample local beverages. The most prevalent options include coffee shops, but breweries and wineries abound in some areas as well.

Coffee Shops

Towns both small and large boast unique coffee shops, and even a ten-minute visit will provide insights into the character and ways of the town you're visiting that you won't get anywhere else. Each projects its own vibe as you enter, and, similar to a farmer's market, a coffee shop serves as a window into the town at large. Are the folks friendly? Is the décor inviting, making you want to sink into a comfy chair with a good book?

One of my favorite "tells" about a good coffee shop is the

glassware in which they serve their beverages and the plates on which they serve their food. In my opinion, the care taken to make me feel both welcomed and invited to linger is in the details, not just the quality of the food and beverages themselves.

Coffee (and tea) seems to make people happy. In these bean-scented oases, we tend to feel a bit of camaraderie, somehow more convivial, more likely to strike up an easy conversation with a barista or patron. So ease in, breathe deeply, and enjoy a few moments to slow down, eyes wide open, and take in all the good smells. You may just find a bit of wonder as you wrap your hands around a warm mug and sip a bit of joy.

Wineries and Breweries

In the last few decades, wineries and breweries have sprung up in both city and country. Much like coffee shops, they provide easy opportunities for conversation, as well as education. Most include tasting rooms where you can learn about what they grow and sample a bit of everything before making a choice to buy a glass or a bottle. In eastern states like New York and Virginia, as well as the better-known vineyard-rich states of California, Oregon, and Washington, time spent at a winery lends itself to gorgeous mountain views, often great small-plate offerings, and wonderful wines.

Even if you're not the type to find wonder in a great cabernet or IPA, many locations boast beautiful picnic areas, hiking trails, and live music, and are often dog friendly.

Novelist Jonathan Safran Foer said, "Food is not rational. Food is culture, habit, craving, and identity." That rings true, and I would amend the sentiment to include "food *and drink*." Take with you what keeps you comfortable and focused on wonder. Stop and revel in new discoveries as you go. Drink that milkshake, eat the lobster roll, savor the shrimp and grits, and let food become part of your adventure!

**Additional food and drink tips, resources, and information can be found at:
www.wonderbingtravel.com/book-resources**

Chapter 16

The Essentials of Safety

My personal list of intangible blessings grows with the advent of every adventure. Joy, wonder, and beauty may be the most celebrated, but they are all underscored with an ever-evolving understanding of personal strength, peace, satisfaction and even accomplishment. I'm drawn into closer communion with the God who loves me and made me as I seek and find

Him in the glory of His creation. Each day dawns shrouded in a bit of mystery, unfolding slowly and deliberately. I pray for eyes, mind, and heart wide open to drink it all in.

The romance is real. The wonder palpable. And though far less miraculous, a more tangible awareness is necessary as well. Traveling alone as a female requires a measure of diligence and preparation as well as a commitment to heightened attention to our surroundings. Our eyes must be open to notice more than wonder, though it remains forever at the forefront. Committing time to consider safety issues may not be glamorous, but this small investment ensures we won't sacrifice joy and wonder because of poor preparation or fear.

I discussed the topic of safety with solo road-tripping friends as well as those who have not yet embarked on their first journey. I discovered that while we share similar concerns, the disparity from one person's comfort and security level to the next can be significant. One of the fun byproducts of solo travel is learning what works for you and only you. Your opinion is the only one that matters! As you work through this chapter, pick and choose what resonates. This is not intended to be a comprehensive instruction manual for safety, but rather an array of suggestions based on years of my own experience and contributions from other travelers and aspiring road-trippers. I share these ideas to create awareness and bring potential situations and solutions to your attention. As you read, you will likely think of alternatives that better fit your needs.

Discussing safety and potential pitfalls isn't intended to create anxiety or concern, but rather increase knowledge so you can move forward confidently (and provide some reassurance for those who love you and know you're heading out on your own). As a solo female traveler, it would be foolish not to purposefully prepare for your own safety and have backup plans if things go sideways!

Safeguard Your Peace of Mind

Road trips, especially those of the longer variety, necessitate mobilizing your whole little world. When we are at home, our access to physical, financial, and emotional help is all nearby. On the road, we are separated from much of that security. While it's unlikely that you'll encounter significant difficulties, it's best to prepare. There are simple precautions and safeguards to help smooth out the potential rough spots.

Managing and prepping your safety "stuff" inevitably involves a bit of paperwork pain the first time you are setting yourself up, but peace of mind will free you up to engage more fully in the joy of your journey. While pausing now to consider "worst case scenarios" may feel as though I'm driving you away from wonder, it is time well spent. If you lose your wallet mid-journey or your car or hotel room are broken into or your phone is broken or missing, it will be too late to come up with a plan. If you're in some type of accident and can't speak for yourself, how will people know who you are or how to help you? Even if you're a fly-by-the-seat-of-your-pants kind of girl, a little thought and preparation at this stage can make an enormous impact on your adventure.

With that in mind, let's approach all this with a bit of perspective, provided by Babs Hoffman: "Stop worrying about the potholes in the road and enjoy the journey." It's wise to be aware of the potholes, but let's not permit them to become the focus of our story. I believe we can take a responsible approach without sucking all the wonder out of the journey before we even start! We want to approach each bend in the road with excited anticipation, not dread.

Securing Your Essentials

I wholeheartedly support leaving the crown jewels at home. Unless your road trip includes a black-tie event, the diamonds and pearls are better left in the jewelry box. As much as you may love your best jewelry, it's likely not essential to your trip. There are, however, certain valuable necessities we cannot successfully travel without. Your credit or debit card, keys, cash, your phone—you simply gotta have 'em, and you need a plan for each if they go missing. My basic rule is to never ever keep all my valuables in the same place. I can work around losses of individual items, but losing everything at once quickly becomes a disaster.

My approach to this tends to alter a little with every adventure I take. I'm always learning how to do better! At this point I do feel confident that my advance preparations will keep me and my belongings from harm, and I have a plan if things go wrong.

Over time, I have settled on a simple approach that divides my essentials into a few different groups. Those categories are dependent on two things: how often I need access to the item and how secure it needs to be. Additionally, my method creates separate spaces for each group of essentials. Here's a short overview, with more explanation added at the end of the section.

24-7 Access

Priority goes to those items I need frequently and immediately several times a day. My general rule of thumb is to never be without these, even if I'm just making a 2-minute pit stop. When I'm on the road, I'm in and out of my vehicle countless times, so I keep it simple, including in this category only those items of ultimate importance.

Your list may differ slightly as you figure out your own level of comfort when walking away from your car to explore, spend the night somewhere, or even just get gas or go to the restroom! The items I keep with me 24/7 include:

- Phone
- Credit or debit card
- Driver's license
- Car key

Personally, I do not feel the need to take a purse when I road trip, and I minimize what I carry around with me. I prefer to have a phone case that either has a magnetic sleeve on the back to hold my credit card and driver's license, or one that has a similar pocket built in. Either option holds only my license and credit card, but they're all I need, and it makes it super simple to grab my phone (with the cards attached) and my keys.

Notes:
- Wherever I may be sleeping, these items remain within grabbing distance should the need arise. I don't want to be fumbling for them in case of an emergency.

- I leave all other keys at home except for my house key, which I tuck into my car console.

Easy Access

I keep these items in my vehicle where I can easily collect them when needed. I do, however, tuck them safely out of sight. I may not need them all, but it's best to have them close by when the need arises. I typically store them in an envelope either in my center console or glove box.

- Health insurance card
- A printed itinerary
- A small amount of cash
- Medical information

Note: Do NOT include anything that would be valuable to a thief if your car was broken into or stolen, such as credit cards, significant amounts of cash, etc.

"In Case of Emergency" Access

Chances are you'll never need this, but it's better to be prepared. In the event you are involved in an accident and not able to provide information for yourself, keep an envelope in your glove box or center console marked, *"In case of emergency, please open."*

Put the following in the envelope:

- A copy of your health insurance card
- A list of emergency contacts
- Any pertinent medical information, including list and location of medications, diabetes or other health info, etc.
- Name and phone of any pertinent doctors

Top Secret Access

It's important to have a "secret" place in your vehicle to keep items that are for your eyes only, and even then, only needed in case of emergencies. Several years ago, I purchased a locked slash-proof bag that I can hide in my car. It has a loop that allows me to attach it around a permanent part of the interior of my SUV (like a metal bar under a back seat). I can easily remove it and carry it into a destination, but I tend to leave it in the car unless I'm staying for a length of time with a friend or family member.

The lists below include items needed if my phone, driver's license, or wallet are lost.

Paperwork (copy both front and back of all cards)

- Copy of main credit/debit card
- Copy of driver's license/passport
- Copy of health insurance cards
- Financial institution's contact information
- Emergency contacts
- Login information to access email, banking, cell phone provider, etc.

Other items

- Spare car key
- Cash
- Additional credit or debit card
- A small backup stash of any important medication

If this feels like overkill to you, then absolutely create a plan that works better for your needs. I've developed my approach over the course of many road trips, and it works for me.

I am a confident traveler, but please know that part of that confidence comes from what I believe to be wise planning. It's easy to jump in the car with a phone and a credit card and be on my way, but I've learned there are too many holes in that short-sighted plan, especially if I am traveling far from home and for longer periods of time.

Consider this next bit my defense for some of the more conservative items in my safety kit!

Money

While most of us use credit and debit cards almost exclusively these days, it is wise to carry some cash on a road trip. There are still some establishments who only deal in cash, and if you're in a situation without electricity, no credit card is going to help. Cash is also great for tips and tolls, grower's markets, and as I learned yesterday, a great little local ice cream shop! If you camp, inevitably you'll need cash for firewood and possibly quarters for coin-operated showers. The more off the beaten path you roam, the more likely you'll encounter vendors who only accept cash. You may come home with the same $100 you left with, but when the need arises you don't want to be without!

Whether you carry cash or a debit or credit card, never be separated from access to money. I carry one credit card with me wherever I go. No matter how I'm choosing to explore, a form of payment always goes with me. Even if I'm hiking in the wilderness, it's on my person or in my hiking bag. If my car is missing when I return, I still have purchasing power in my pocket. I never want to get in a situation where I could be separated from everything.

In my hidden emergency safety pouch, I always include a photocopy of my main credit or debit card. If the card is stolen or compromised, I have what I need to call the bank. (Be sure to photocopy both sides, ensuring you have the phone number, expiration date, and CID code.)

I always have an alternate card stashed away in my pouch in case the main card is lost or compromised in any way.

In case of theft (either of what you're carrying with you

personally or what's in your car or place of lodging), always call the bank or credit card company as soon as you are missing your card. Keep in mind the bank will shut down your card immediately, which will protect you from potential rogue charges. However, you also lose the ability to use it not only in person but for any future reservations you may have made later in your trip. A great justification for carrying a backup card!

Extra Car Key

Losing your car key is the worst. Always travel with a backup key!

I keep my backup key fob in my safety pouch, though that can be problematic in cars that start with a remote fob and not an inserted key. My car starts remotely as long as a key fob is physically in the car, which means that even if my spare is hidden in my pouch, anyone who might break in can start the car. Some people swear by hiding a key magnetically under the vehicle or in the wheel well, but as I drive plenty of bumpy back roads, that makes me nervous. Instead, I pop it into my safety pouch, but I remove the battery first, and keep the key and battery together in a small Ziploc bag. The car won't start if broken into, and the key is stored safely inside the car.

Managing with and without Your Smart Phone

Cell phones have forever altered the way we handle information. For good or bad, they offer us instant access to almost every important piece of data in our lives. As wonder-seeking road-trippers, we want to minimize the use of our phones as entertainment while taking full advantage of their powerful ability to guide and ease our travels. Access to directions, restaurant and lodging referrals, hiking trails, and operating hours all enhance our adventures. The amazing capabilities of our smart phones can enrich our experiences. Technology on a road trip can be such a gift—such a time-saver! Until it's not.

The thought of being "phoneless" sends ripples of panic into many of us, especially when we travel. I learned this fear has a name—NOMOPHOBIA. While the condition is intended to describe a more irrational anxiety, the fear of disconnection is a reasonable one for solo travelers. We worry about breaking or losing our phones, having them stolen, forgetting chargers, and losing access to service or power. So much of what we need when we are traveling is on our phones: itineraries, GPS, access to people, access to money, weather, camera. Life in our pockets. But we need to be prepared for the possibility of losing it all.

Backup Plans

Without a phone, you lose access to essential information. Have a hard copy backup plan! Here is a list of things I print out to pop into my safety pouch:

1. Emergency contact information
2. The phone number of my bank
3. Login information for:
    a. online banking
    b. email
    c. cell phone provider
    d. Venmo or PayPal if you have them. This is

an easy way to receive money from a trusted person if you have a crisis

e. Facebook and Instagram. If you have no way to text, using the Messenger app will allow you to communicate with family members or friends

4. My itinerary

I am days away from embarking on a two-week (maybe more?) road trip through upstate New York, Vermont and Quebec. I'm excited! I've also planned a little more than usual, partly because I'm crossing an international line, and partly because almost everywhere I go will be new. Since I'll be traipsing through areas with minimal lodging options, and I don't want to get stuck with no room at the inn, I have made several reservations in advance. There's also the issue of spotty and unpredictable cell service in the mountains and across the Canadian border. Printing out a hard copy of everything is key to my peace and increases my ability to relax and let all the wonder of the Adirondack and Green Mountains wash over me. Once across the border I'll struggle a bit with my rusty French, so having things on paper to show people will be a help!

5. Before you embark on your big adventure, create a folder full of wonderfully cumbersome paper that includes the following:

a. Every reservation you have made—be sure contact info, destination address and phone number, as well as confirmation is included.

b. Contact information for any people you plan to connect with—name, address, phone, and email if it makes sense!

    c. Names and addresses of any mini-destinations you may need, such as parks, museums, stores, restaurants, etc.

    d. If you're traveling for many days and have advance plans to drive to certain areas or definitive destinations, type up a short schedule for yourself. Whether you adhere to it or not is completely up to you, but I find it helpful to see it laid out in front of me.

Technology Tips

Smart Phone doom and gloom aside, let's assume you and your device remain connected throughout your travels. Your smart phone (as well as your smart watch if you have one) can serve you well if you encounter trouble in other areas. Here are a few safety measures that ensure both are working for you while you travel.

Setting Up Emergency Contacts

You should absolutely have designated emergency contacts set up as such in your phone. Whether you are an iPhone or Android user, the process is similar for adding one or several contacts who can be notified quickly and easily. A quick Google or YouTube search will provide instructions. Once you designate your emergency contacts, here are some cool features you may not be aware of.

Medical ID

Emergency information can be accessed on any iPhone by pressing and holding the side button and a volume button, and then sliding the Medical ID button. The screen will show pertinent info about yourself including age, allergies, blood type, height and weight, as well as names and phone numbers for your emergency contacts. You can even add your vision prescription! The Health app on your phone allows you to update all this information at any time.

If you wear an Apple Watch, the same information is available simply by pressing the side button (below the dial) and holding it in.

911

Using the same method as above, you (or someone else) can activate the 911 option on your phone. On an iPhone, simply push the same two buttons you use for the Medical ID but slide the SOS Emergency Call option. The procedure for an Apple Watch is exactly the same. This option not only allows you (or a person who may not have your phone password) to access emergency services, but sends an alert with your current location to all emergency cell number contacts. The process for Android users is slightly different; just press the power button five times in a row to alert 911.

Lock Screen

When traveling, be sure to keep your phone password protected. While you need access at all times, you certainly don't want to unwittingly provide your information to anyone else, even for a moment.

Password Protection

We all keep a list of passwords somewhere handy. You'll likely need access to a few of these in your travels, and it's impossible to remember usernames and passwords for everything from banking to Netflix! Chances are you have a file somewhere. If you keep that information on your phone, be sure the file itself is protected, or add a password manager app to ensure only you can unlock the login information.

Find My iPhone/Find My Mobile

It's crucial that at least one person on this earth knows how to find you at all times. If you don't already use this feature on your phone/watch/laptop, I suggest adding the app and setting it up in advance of your trip. As a solo traveler, I want my kids to be able to locate me if I am not answering my phone. It provides all of us extra peace of mind, and it's easy and non-intrusive. They can look and see where I'm located without having to text or call.

In addition to location services, the app has several other helpful features. You can:

a. Mark your phone as lost, which locks your device to prevent others from accessing it

b. Remotely erase your phone if you fear it has been stolen and your information compromised

c. Ping your phone if you've misplaced it so that a consistent loud noise plays for several seconds

d. Connect your watch and laptop to the app. If any of your smart devices are lost or stolen, all the same information applies. Just remember that you will need to gain access to your account to enact these services. That's simple enough if you lose your phone but have your laptop, or vice versa. But if you need to use another person's phone or laptop, you'll need to know your Apple ID and password to gain access through icloud.com/find

Both the android and Apple "find my" apps are very user friendly. A quick look will provide you with all the options.

Online Safety and Prep

We've explored many of the ups and downs of traveling with technology, but here are a few more tips to help keep you, your technology, and your content safe while you're on the road:

- If you plan to post about your travels on social media, do not post in real time. Part of the fun of posting when you're on the road is to share a wonderful place or experience with those who follow you, but delay your post until you are no longer in that location. Hashtags and location services make it easy for viewers to see where the photos were taken, and it's best to play it safe and be long gone when the post is live.

- Be sure you have your phone and your laptop backed up to the Cloud or on an external drive before you leave on your trip.

- If you plan to take oodles of photos, determine how much free space you have on your phone. You don't want to spend hours mid-adventure deleting old photos and texts to make room for all the new memories you want to preserve.

- Make sure your phone is in good working order. There are apps available that will run a health check for you!

- Pack an extra charger, but also a power bank/portable charger for those moments when you may not have access to an outlet or phone jack. To ensure all your devices can be powered up, purchase one that has inputs for USB, your phone, and a lightning jack.

Car Care

Since our vehicles are literally the driving force of our adventures, ensuring we can depend on them as well as protect them is paramount to our peace on the road. Before you ever leave home, there are several ways to set yourself up for success in your travels.

1. Take your car to a trusted mechanic or dealership to have it thoroughly checked out before you leave. If you're going to be driving thousands of miles, this should be non-negotiable. Most service departments will check and/or change your oil and other fluids, ensure your tires are in good condition, rotate and balance your tires, and check your brakes. You can ask for a multi-point inspection as well, which will dive a little deeper. At minimum these typically include checking wiper blades, interior and exterior lights, your battery life, and turn signals. If your car is older or hasn't been checked recently, consider opting for a more thorough inspection.

2. Know how to change a tire. If you've never done it, you can easily learn! Before you leave home, ask a friend or relative to demonstrate for you, and video the process on your phone. YouTube provides plenty of options for how-to videos as well. You can even search for a YouTube video of your specific vehicle. I found one that walks me through every detail and is specific to my car. Regardless of how you prepare, you'll need to know how to do each of the following:

   a. access your spare tire, jack, and tools

   b. use your jack

c. remove the spare tire from its well

d. remove the flat tire from the car

e. attach and secure the spare tire

None of these is particularly difficult, and it's worth practicing before you leave home. Being stuck on the side of the road is unnerving, but if you can take control of the situation and change your own tire, you can drive to a service station without having to rely on significant and potentially expensive help.

3. Invest in a roadside assistance program. While we tend to think primarily of AAA, many car insurance policies also provide towing, help if you lock your keys in the car, and other emergency support. If you own a General Motors vehicle, you may already have the OnStar system built in, which provides additional safety and security measures.

4. Always travel with a spare key for your car. I know it may seem slightly counterintuitive to have both keys with you, but if you're 500 miles from home, knowing the spare is safely in your kitchen junk drawer isn't going to help you.

5. Start each day with a full tank of gas, especially if you're traveling into rural areas.

6. Know your license plate. If your car were to be stolen, that is the first question you'd be asked and many of us would be hard-pressed to provide an accurate response! Take a photo of your license plate and keep it in your phone.

7. Ensure your registration and inspection are both up to date, and that your insurance card and vehicle registration cards are in the glove compartment. It's worth having a copy of both of these on your phone as well.

Emergency Items

No explanations needed here. This is my list of "must have" items that go with me when I travel. A breakdown of my first aid and tool kits is included in the resources at the end of the chapter.

- Personal
    - First Aid Kit
    - 2-3 gallon-jugs of water
    - Extra pair of glasses
    - Sunglasses
    - Healthy snack food
    - Sunscreen
    - Bug spray
- Vehicle
    - Cordless pump for tires
    - Jumper cables
    - Flares
- Technology
    - Backup chargers
    - Power pack
- Other
    - Light-up sticks
    - Rope
    - Basic tool kit

En Route Tips and Safety

Not all safety measures can be anticipated before your journey begins. You may still encounter some unexpected bumps and mishaps along the way. Here are a few tips that may be the difference between confidence and concern in the midst of your journey.

Personal Safety

It's important to portray an air of confidence when you travel. It's likely you'll have moments when you feel less than sure of yourself, but there's no need to share that with others either verbally or with your body language. Sending signals of uncertainty or insecurity to those you encounter may lead to unwanted attention and curiosity. In addition to the previously shared technology tips, here are a few safety pointers that help me feel more confident as well as safe.

- Carry a whistle and/or mace. While I've never had cause to use either, carrying a mini version of both on my lanyard with my car key definitely boosts my confidence, especially when I'm hiking and camping.

- Appear confident and in control when dealing with others. Obvious indecision signals a lack of self-assurance. If you need to "fake it until you make it," intentionally adopt a no-nonsense firm manner, confident facial expression, and businesslike voice. You can be polite without being wishy washy!

- Know where you are. Pay attention to your geography. What town did you just pass through? What road are you on? Your GPS is not a replacement for your brain! It's important that you have enough locational awareness to provide basic information in an emergency situation.

- Travel in the daylight and get yourself settled before dark. This allows you to take stock of your surroundings. Let's face it. We're all more confident in the light of day.

- Keep your eyes open to your surroundings. Of course wonder is the goal, but as a solo female traveler, you must pay attention to what's going on around you. After a bit of practice, this becomes second nature. Besides, you don't want to miss anything on this journey!

- Check the weather forecast each morning. Getting blindsided by unexpected storms, heat, or severe cold can absolutely dampen your spirits as well as put you in danger.

- If any situation makes you nervous, go with your gut. That may mean driving away from a restaurant or hotel, or turning around on a street or path where you are walking. If it feels funky, call someone on your phone to "walk" or "drive" with you as you leave the situation. And keep that mace and whistle with you!

- Arrange a check-in with someone at least once a day, if cell service allows.

Lodging Safety

There are quite a few little things you can do to enhance your sense of security during a solo stay at a hotel or Airbnb. We all want that happy feeling when we enter our room for the night and close the door. Here are a few tips to ensure a feeling of peace.

1. Before making a reservation, read lots of reviews. Always.

2. If you're renting a home or cabin, etc., confirm the type of property. Are you renting a room in a larger

home or do you have the entire place to yourself? Personally, I only stay where I am renting the entire space as I do not feel comfortable renting a room with shared areas, though you may be more comfortable with others closeby.

3. "See" the property. Check out all online photos and utilize Google Earth to get a sense of how the property is situated in the area. You can see how close the parking lot is to the entrance, if the surroundings are pleasant, etc. If you do not have an exact address before booking, you may need to ask for more detail from the property owner.

4. When you reserve a hotel room, consider

   a. requesting an upper floor

   b. making the reservation for two people

   c. requesting a room that does not have a connecting door

   d. asking for a room away from the stairwell

5. Ask how the parking area is lit after dark.

6. Take a small rubber doorstop with you. You can wedge it under your door to ensure that no one can physically open the door.

Personal Checklist

Those few moments prior to departing each day are filled with anticipation for the day ahead, and potentially a bit of confusion as I pile my things back into the car after a short stay. I've learned how imperative it is to take a moment to ensure I have everything before I set out. What works best for me is to create a short mental list of items I never want to leave without. Mine isn't complicated. I run through this list each day before I start the car.

- Phone
- Keys
- Laptop
- Credit/Debit card
- Driver's license
- Dog ☺
- Glasses/Sunglasses

And now, a deep breath, everyone! This land of safety measures and worst-case scenarios is not where we choose to dwell, though investing a bit of time and thought into positioning yourself strongly will provide more peace and confidence in your adventure. The joy is in the journey after all! File away what resonates with you, what gives you solace and confidence. You will make your own path in this area, picking and choosing what works best for you and your unique brand of travel and wonder. It's time to pack your bags!

The world is waiting for you. Good Luck. Travel Safe. Go!

—Phil Keoghan

Additional safety tips, resources, and information can be found at:
www.wonderbingtravel.com/book-resources

Chapter 17

Packing

Travel is about the gorgeous feeling of teetering in the unknown.

—Anthony Bourdain

You have almost everything you need to embark on your first solo adventure! This last bit of organizing and packing marks the final mission standing between you and the thrill of the first turn out of the driveway. For some, this last task triggers eager anticipation, but I recognize that others have a long-standing hate relationship with packing for any trip. Keep your goals of freedom and wonder at the forefront; it will lessen any pain. In the pages ahead we will walk the highwire between necessary planning and moving blissfully forward into "the gorgeous feeling of teetering in the unknown."

Gathering and organizing all the necessities for a road trip means mobilizing your little world, which may feel daunting. However, it can be simplified into three basics tasks: determine what you need, add what you want, and organize it well enough that you don't lose your marbles on Day Two, searching in vain for your socks, backup charger, or that bag of gummy worms you've been saving. It all comes down to basic organization and a bit of forethought.

Don't Forget Freedom

In the opening pages of this guide, I shared with you how the intentional act of road-tripping provides unending opportunities to find freedom. We've explored many manifestations of this concept—freedom *from* regular life, but more intentionally freedom *to* see, hear, think, and experience life more clearly and fully as we seek the wonder of God in the glory of His creation.

How can packing for our journey possibly serve to fulfil this mission? Like so many of the practical endeavors we've explored, packing well truly liberates us from focusing on the mundane so that we can fully embrace the sublime.

Freedom from Restriction

We can identify this as "freedom from restriction" or, simply stated, freedom to take whatever you want! Since you're not hopping a plane to cross the continent or ocean, there are neither restrictions nor limitations to what you take and no fee for packing a large item or suitcase. Unless you're driving a Smart Car, you'll have room for a healthy dose of excess, should that be your desire. While I think that's exciting, I realize some women prefer the constraints of a defined space, like a suitcase. Actual luggage keeps items orderly and limits the overwhelm when determining what to pack. Both approaches are possible. Whether you are a minimalist or a "take all the things" kind of girl, you get to determine what you need and what makes you comfortable and confident. Yours is the freedom to decide what will provide you with peace.

No matter your approach, it will take some time to find your sweet spot between excess and the bare minimum. I can relate to both. I've worked hard to become a minimalist when I'm flying, and it's been a worthy venture. However, all my finely honed skills in packing light swiftly fly out the window at the sight of my SUV, rear hatch stretched wide open and welcoming, tempting me to take all the things. And so I do. Sort of.

I have found freedom in a happy balance. Yes, I can take anything I want, but over the years, I've learned that over-packing adds stress. I don't always do packing well, and it's an ongoing lesson. The ultimate goal is to be unencumbered by too much "stuff" yet have everything I truly need. When the proportion is just right, whatever I have brought along with me ultimately serves to complement the goal of seeking wonder. That's the sweet spot.

Freedom of Packing for One

I find great joy in knowing that every blessed thing I put in my vehicle goes only because I want it there. While that may sound a bit selfish, this is truly one of the pleasures of solo travel. If you've ever traveled with children, a significant other, parents, siblings, even friends—you understand. In all those scenarios, some sharing is assumed. That's all well and good, but let your mind wander a bit to imagine claiming all the cup holders, choosing your own podcasts and music, and stopping only when *you* need a restroom. Not to mention, your hair bands and lip balm are actually your hair bands and lip balm.

I also find it gratifying that no one is going to move my stuff. No one will "borrow" my charger, favorite sweatshirt, or sunglasses. All the goodies are mine, and no one is hiding, borrowing, or leaving anything behind. There's no shame in celebrating the freedom to choose what I pack and claiming it as mine for the duration of the experience. While hardly a lofty thought, I believe wholeheartedly there is wonder even in this!

We want to ensure wonder stays at the forefront, even as we sort and plot and plan what to take with us. Packing for a road trip does not need to be complicated and investing a bit of time to consider what will work for you will pay dividends while you're on the road. If the prospect feels overwhelming, be encouraged. A little organization will ensure you'll soon have it all stacked and packed and ready for wonder.

Creative Space

Take a five-minute walk through any busy airport or train station, and the experience will be relatively unchanged from New York's Penn Station to LAX. Everyone's checking a bag or wheeling a suitcase through the terminal, usually with a carry-on slung over their shoulder. Nice and neat, everything crammed into the little space permitted. This is the necessary order of air and train travel, though hardly a model for creativity and individualism. But packing for a road trip is an entirely different sport, as unique as it is personal.

I have admired and marveled at the methods of others over the years, wondering at their approach to the art of packing it all and gleaning bits and pieces of both genius and insanity. Some enterprising people build entire organizational structures in the back of their vans and SUVs, complete with shelving and cubbies for every little item. At the other extreme, I've been at rest areas and watched folks open their tailgates only to throw themselves at the heaps and piles within, attempting to stay the impending avalanche of stuff. Both inspire awe!

Many years ago, while packing for a short road trip with a close college friend, I learned what has proven to be my most favorite packing hack. Allow me to introduce you to the magic of the laundry basket. Unless my friend is flying, the basket is her "suitcase" of choice. I love this so much and have adopted this philosophy almost 100% of the time I am traveling by car, though I alter the strategy a bit for longer road trips. Packing my clothing and toiletries, hair dryer (and even shoes on short trips) is now incredibly freeing. So much room! No zipping or stuffing! This simple idea has informed so many of my organizational choices over the years. I'll share in more detail shortly, as I know you're intrigued!

Another road-tripping friend owns an older conversion van she fondly refers to as "Roger." When she feels it's about time for an adventure, she starts getting Roger ready and packs her suitcase so she can go at a moment's notice. Her van has a little closet permanently full of clothes, and when the mood strikes, she takes off. I love the idea of pre-packing when the time for a road trip is drawing near. It's so much easier to leave on a whim!

I share all this to help you tap into your own creativity and allow it to work for you. This is your trip. You can be as creative or traditional with your packing as you like. There are no rules. The ultimate focus here is to help you brainstorm your way to taking what you want and need and organizing it in a way that works for you.

The Basics

There are two major components to packing for a road trip. The first stage of packing is preparation—deciding what to take, purchasing needed items, and gathering the things you already own. Once complete, the remaining process is purely organizational—choosing luggage, coolers, and other containers, filling them with the appropriate items, and finally packing it all in your vehicle in a way that provides easy access and security for all your belongings.

The pages ahead provide practical help for managing both steps. I'll suggest categories of things to consider taking with you, and you can fill in the particulars. You'll find specifics lists and ideas in the resources if you'd like more details. As always, you are free to pick and choose what resonates!

Organization

Ultimately, each of our approaches to organization and our level of comfort with it will be unique. Finding your sweet spot in this area will enhance your ability to wonder freely. At a very base level, we can consider two extremes: those that resonate with the mantra "bless this mess" or with its antithesis, "mess = stress." As with most polarities, the happy place for most of us lies somewhere in the middle. Wherever you land, remember that how you choose to manage your "stuff" should enhance your adventure, not add anxiety to it.

The concept of organization relates to so many different

elements of packing. At its most basic, it means having a plan that works for you for your entire adventure. On a more granular level, it relates to your choice of containers, where you choose to store items for ease of access, and your overall plan to keep track of everything.

It's worth investing a bit of time and effort to do this well. Creating a system that allows you to remain organized after days on the road is more important than simply starting out with a beautifully packed back seat and trunk. Mauling through all your containers and bags in search of your extra water bottle or sunscreen is the worst. However you pack it all up, it doesn't have to look pretty. It just needs to work for you. I call this being "comfortably organized." Let's begin with the uber practical and tactical.

Containers

This may seem overly simple, but *how* I store everything is the most important component to remaining organized for the course of my adventure. Over time I've found that keeping everything possible in clear plastic containers makes it simple to find what I need and to organize it well before I go. It's easy to let things get messy mid-trip, but just popping loose items into their proper bucket or bin is enough to ensure things remain neat and organized.

My big-picture overview of how I store all my road-tripping needs fits into three categories of storage: plastic bins, other containers, and items large enough to store on their own.

Plastic Bins

I use exclusively clear bins so I can easily see the contents, though they vary in size according to need. For example, my camping and non-perishable food bins are quite large, but my first aid kit and personal items need only small containers. Most have lids, but not all. I love having a bin where I can toss all my shoes, especially if it's a little messy outside. This approach makes it easy to locate and grab the first aid kit or the paper towels, a clean pair of socks, etc. For my personal bathroom items, I have two containers: one make-up-style bag and one caddy for shower needs. It's easy to grab and go!

Additional Containers

Bins aren't a logical solution for everything. In addition to necessary cooler(s), different sized garbage bags come in handy for trash, dirty clothing, and wet shoes. I carry a soft zippered storage bag to hold my pillow, sheets and towels, or any other linen-related items I may need while camping. This keeps them clean and dry, which becomes increasingly important the longer I'm on the road! I always carry some sort of overnight bag or backpack that will hold a small amount of clothing, and maybe most importantly, an organizer that fits on my front seat. I'll share more details on these items shortly.

Non-container Items:

This last group includes mostly camping-related items, such as my tent, sleeping bag, air mattress, camp chair, etc. They're all larger items that can easily exist on their own or have their own bag. If you're not a camper, then lucky you! You'll have that much more room for on-the-road shopping and packing all those items we tend to bring along "just in case."

Container Tips: *Let's drill down a bit into a few of my favorite creative container tips.*

The Laundry Basket

My favorite packing hack for clothing, I use this not just on long road trips, but on any journey where I'm traveling by car and want the freedom to pack whatever clothes I wish. On lengthier road trips, I've actually upgraded to a long but shallow clear plastic container with a lid that snaps, but the philosophy is unchanged. My SUV has a "secret" storage area in the back where the entire container fits out of sight, ensuring everything remains cool and dry while preventing dirt and dampness. I roll my clothes, Marie Kondo-style, so I can easily see everything and grab what I need.

I know you're likely thinking it would be odd (and inconvenient) to show up at a hotel with a giant laundry basket or bin holding all your clothing. That's the other glorious half of the hack. The bin stays in the car at all times. I carry a small overnight bag, half-filled with all my socks and underthings. If I'm staying for a few nights at a hotel or Airbnb or visiting friends and family, I pull out needed clothes from the basket or bin and pop them into the overnight bag. I can easily walk into my lodgings with a small bag containing everything I want, while leaving everything I do not need in the car during my stay. As dirty clothes pile up, they are transferred to a garbage bag and back into the bin, safely separate from the clean clothing.

Mini Chest of Drawers

Several years ago, I bought a small, plastic 3-drawer vertical unit to pop in the back of my SUV. It provides easy access to a variety of items. I like it because it's stable and takes up only a small amount of floor space. How I utilize the unit changes from trip to trip.

Because I tend to camp several times on my longer road trips, often this storage unit contains items for camping. I've used it, too, as a dresser to store socks and underwear, pairs of flip flops, or even snacks. I also find that, as the days go by, little items I don't know what to do with surface and need a home, not to mention small gifts and goodies purchased along the way. These drawers are a wonderful place to pop miscellaneous items for safekeeping. I will confess that one of these drawers typically takes on the role of "junk drawer" by the end of the trip. Much like in my kitchen, little items materialize that just don't seem to fit anywhere else!

Front Seat Organizer

If there's one organizational item I can't imagine traveling without, this is it. Perhaps it's the teacher in me who loves all things related to hoarding and organizing school supplies, but one of the best purchases I made before my first big road trip was a car organizer. My little buddy sits on the front passenger seat and provides me with quick access to all the things I need en route. While it holds items you'd typically put into a satchel or backpack, the compartments vary in size and are open for easy viewing. The organizer snaps around the headrest of the front seat so it won't go flying, and I can disconnect it and sling it over my shoulder when I arrive at my destination.

Many versions of front seat buddies are available online. I've included some specific suggestions in the resources for you! In my particular version, I have all this at my fingertips:

- Folder with printed itinerary, reservations, etc.
- Maps
- Composition book*
- Chargers
- Laptop
- Glasses
- Flashlight
- Journals
- Devotional
- Kindle/book
- Earbuds

*I purchase and utilize a new composition book for every trip. It is my basic trip planner, where I have brainstormed ideas from the inception stage, and where I sketch out in advance what I may know about each day of the journey. While on the road, I keep it close at hand to track my gas and mileage, as well as spending. It's not fancy, and a bit of a mess from sketching ideas, working through the length of my trip, etc. In hindsight, these have proven to be wonderful resources for me when I need to review details of previous trips. Over the years I've collected quite a stack of them, and each hold plenty of their own memories of wonder.

Before you purchase your own version of the front seat organizer, consider all that you wish to have access to during your driving time, any paperwork you may need upon arrival at your evening destination, and electronics or other small valuables you'd like to easily carry into your lodging for the evening. The organizers come in many sizes and can serve slightly different purposes, so take time to consider what would work best for you.

Tips for Packing It All Up

The purpose of each of these tips and thoughts is simply to ensure that packing serves you; it should not rule you. Once you're on the road, packing and organization fade into the background, supporting actors to your ability to seek wonder and providing freedom for days of joyful exploration. As you read through, consider what appeals to your sense of organization and adventure!

- **Packing List:** An actual printed packing list serves me well. I divide it into categories, such as "food for cooler," "clothing," "camping," etc. I save the document on my computer, which makes it easy to add and subtract items from trip to trip. It also helps me determine how much room might be needed for each group of items. I check each item twice: once to confirm I have pulled out and packed each article in its container followed by a second check when I've loaded it into my vehicle.

- **Spreading it all out:** Before I physically load my vehicle, I carry everything into a common space, like my foyer or driveway. This gives me a last look at the whole lot of it. I can usually tell if I've overdone it and need to pare things down a bit or consolidate certain items. Spreading it all out also provides a great opportunity to check everything against my packing list.

- **Putting the puzzle together:** Take a few minutes to consider where your packed containers, bins, and miscellaneous items will reside in your vehicle. Especially if you're loading your car to the gills, it's worthwhile having some sort of method to your placement madness.

- **Cheat Sheet:** If you're an excessive organizer, this tip may be for you. I've traveled enough that this info is in my head, but if you're heading out for the first time, especially on a longer adventure, consider creating a little cheat sheet, listing the contents of each container, that you can keep up front with you.

- **Traveling with your dog:** I'll share all my canine travel and packing tips in their very own chapter, but for now consider how much space your furry friend will occupy. Is he or she traveling in a crate in the back, or on a seat? If you're traveling in the summer, be sure to consider proximity to air conditioning vents while you're on the road. They get so much warmer than we do!

- **Campers:** Just an encouragement for those of you planning to do some camping. Inevitably, you'll be traveling with more stuff than the average explorer. Do your best to keep your camping items centrally organized and accessible. It's frustrating to scramble for items when you're setting up camp. While I absolutely love camping, lengthy searches for elusive tent stakes or my flashlight put a huge damper on the evening and my attitude!

- **Day Stops:** If you're planning to stop and explore through the day, consider the items you may need to easily access, like your camera, food for lunch from the cooler, hiking shoes, etc. If I know I'll be stopping for a mid-day hike, I make sure it's easy to grab my hiking bag, shoes, first-aid items, any maps, and extra water before I hit the trail. Lexi the Golden is almost always with me, and she grows impatient rather quickly when she knows we're about to head off into the woods!

- **Coolers and Food:** Before I load food into my vehicle, I divide my stores into a few categories.

  Front Seat:

  - o Small cooler for easy access to cold drinks and snacks
  - o Small bag of unrefrigerated snacks

  Back:

  - o Bin for unrefrigerated foods
  - o Larger cooler for additional cold foods

Other than the perishable factor, determining how to pack your food is just like deciding how to organize anything else you take with you. Consider what you want easy access to while you're driving, what you want to put your hands on quickly when you stop during the day, and those items that you'll only need for overnight stays. If you're camping, you'll likely take more with you! Please refer to the resources for my specific food lists. While your taste will be unique to you, these may spark a few ideas!

Tips for Choosing Your Clothes and Personal Items

If there's one area where I can fall into the overpacking-prone "just in case" trap, it's with clothing and shoes. I've learned a few tricks that help me make better decisions, but I fully admit to being a work in progress in this area. If you relate to my struggles, consider trying these ideas:

1. No matter how long my trip, I take clothes for 6-7 days. If it takes longer than that to get to my des-

tination, I can always find a laundromat to do a quick load.

2. The further I travel, the more likely the climate may change along the way. This does make it harder to be a minimalist. For those necessary items that take up lots of space, I choose things I love and can wear multiple times, such as one jacket or vest, one heavier hooded sweatshirt, one lighter sweatshirt, one pair of jeans, and one versatile pair of pants that I can easily wash out in a sink if necessary. I also pack layers of clothing. My favorite travel "outfit" in the summer is flip flops, a pair of shorts, and a tank top with a long-sleeve shirt over it. If the mornings are quite chilly, I keep a sweatshirt nearby. It's easy to add and subtract layers as needed throughout the day. My specific packing list for clothing provides more details.

3. If I know I'm going to be doing something that requires an outfit I won't need on the rest of my trip, I fully commit to what I'll wear for that event before I pack instead of taking "choices" with me and deciding later.

4. **My most effective tip:** Before you load it into your luggage, lay out every bit of your clothing and shoes so you can see it all. This visual often helps me recognize when I am overdoing it. At this juncture, I intentionally remove at least one item of every type of clothing. I've rarely been sorry to take less!

5. I do take plenty of underclothing. It takes up such a small amount of room, and let's face it, no one wants to run out of clean underwear!

Planning for the Hotel/Airbnb

I'm only too happy to share this hard-learned lesson with you. While one of the great joys of road-tripping means taking whatever you want, one of the great frustrations can be wading through your packed car in search of those few items you need for a one- or two-night stay. I've handled this poorly in the past, resulting in one of two situations. I either end up hauling half of what I own into the hotel for my super short stay, or I try to just grab what I need. The latter always results in many trips back and forth to the car for the thing I forgot, and then the next thing, and the next. If you're traveling with a dog, this becomes more problematic and horribly inconvenient if your dog goes in and out every time you do! Here are a few tips to ensure that you truly enjoy your hotel or Airbnb splurge.

1. When you're still at home, take a moment to think through what you'll need with you in those situations and, later, pack your car with access in mind.

2. This is where the overnight bag holding only necessary clothes and bathroom stuff is key.

3. Frequently, a hotel room or Airbnb will have a refrigerator. When traveling with a cooler full of food, I often use this opportunity to bring my cooler in and pop everything in the fridge/freezer until I leave again.

4. I keep all my electronics (laptop, Kindle, chargers, etc.) in my front-seat organizer, and always take it in with me. Having these items all in one place makes it easy to transport them away from the

front seat where they're easily seen by passers-by or where they can get overheated in summer weather.

It's worth saying again: don't allow packing to stress you out, but, rather, find a happy place through your planning. If the details of what to take and how to pack cause you anxiety, then take a breath. You probably need to step back and view the bigger picture, if only for a moment. The goal in the end is to find freedom on the road, not to be overcome with details or worry about what you've remembered, or what you may have forgotten. And by the way, you will forget something. It won't matter. The experiences, the joy, the tears, and the passion of your journey are what will live with you forever. It will never, ever be what you packed or what you forgot. Hold it all loosely.

Fill your life with experiences, not things. Have stories to tell, not stuff to show.

—Anonymous

Additional packing tips, resources, and information can be found at: www.wonderbingtravel.com/book-resources

Chapter 18

The Missing Pieces:
Faith and Trust

Embarking on a solo road trip provides a unique opportunity to live every moment to its full measure. For a brief time, we leave the labels—mom, daughter, wife, girlfriend, employee, boss—and weightiness of our identity behind us and forge intrepidly ahead, newly branded as explorer, adventurer, seeker of wonder. In the time it takes to close the driver's side door, our time, our plans, and our days transform into our singular treasure.

Even after years of solo road-tripping, I find liberation in that moment of metamorphosis. I relish the freedom to turn my focus on wonder, to move forward as scheduled or unscheduled as I wish to be—eyes open to the endless opportunities for discovery around each bend.

My beloved author Pat Conroy writes eloquently of this moment in his memoir, *My Reading Life*. Blessed with the gift of transforming keen observations into compelling descriptions, he penned this after observing fellow travelers residing in the same Paris hotel where he was staying: "Voyagers can remove the masks and those sinuous, intricate disguises we wear at home in the dangerous equilibrium of our common lives. The men and women I met at the Grand Hôtel des Balcons traveled to change themselves, to trust their bright impulse with the hope they would receive the gift of the sublime, life-changing encounter somewhere on the road. There is no voyage without a spiritual, even religious impulse." While his commentary leans a bit toward the propensity to escape rather than seek wonder, that common desire to seek "the gift of the sublime" rooted in a spiritual . . . impulse speaks directly to the wonderer in me.

Are you beginning to sense the reality of your own journey ahead? Your own freedom and path to wonder? Perhaps even a "life-changing encounter"? I hope you're excited, ready to get on with your planning, and filled with anticipation and hope. Hold on to all that. We've traveled a long way together; you've learned so much and have earned those feelings of expectation. There is much to look forward to, and there will indeed be plenty of wonder in your solo adventuring future.

As we head into the last leg of our journey together, we need to pause for a bit of introspection. Take heart! The goal is encouragement, not bubble bursting. We need to consider those inevitable moments when despite all your efforts to do the best and right things, you will encounter moments of doubt, uncertainty, and possibly fear. What will you do? How do you move forward and do the next right thing? Let's sort through it in the here and now, so you aren't blindsided down the road. As it unfolds, you'll find it's all a matter of faith. And trust.

You Are Trustworthy

You are prepared to tackle most of what you will encounter in your travels. Have confidence and faith in your personal preparation. Embrace all the essential pillars of planning and take advantage of every practical resource provided in these pages. That itself will carry you quite far. Furthermore, from a heart perspective, you know what you're after! You've determined your passions, your tears and treasure. When you marry that with all the practical, you're well on your way to wonder—so close you can touch it.

For all of the above and all that follows here, you are worthy of trust: trust in your intuition, your gut, your innate sense of what is a wise choice. Your solo adventure may be the first time you make a lot of these decisions on your own. Brava! This is great news, and you are up for it. Trust your instincts. If something seems off, lean into that. If you sense danger or fear, move away quickly. You can and should have faith in your abilities, your preparation, and your in-trip decision-making.

Receive this as the confidence booster it is intended to be, but let's not rest here. There is another layer to trust, beyond what we can manage for ourselves.

He Is Trust Worthy

Trust in the Lord with all your heart, and do not lean on your own understanding. In all your ways acknowledge Him, and He will make straight your paths.

Proverbs 3:5, 6

As a Christian, I know that my ability to navigate wonder, to ensure my safety, and to execute every detail involved in my journey isn't really mine at all, but God-granted. While I am worthy of trust, it is my worth as His that enables me to thrive in my adventures. If I depend solely on what I see in the mirror to lead me to joy and wonder, I will fall short, more wanderer than wonderer. Continued faith and trust in the power of the presence of the One who created it all makes the journey all the richer.

And while all this is woven deep into my soul, I still make a mess of things. In those moments when I find myself in over my head, I often leave God's peaceful presence in a heap on the closest curb. I shift quickly to an "I can handle it all by myself" problem-solving mode, and easily make bad choices, acting out of my own strength and a place of fear, before I am reminded yet again that just doesn't cut it. I freeze with doubt, not trusting myself to act yet not inviting God into the moment. I unwittingly leave Him out of the picture, and my poor judgement leads to frustration and confusion.

No matter my best efforts, I will walk this path again. I will make poor choices. But I remind myself that my intention is to seek after Him, watch as He reveals His glory in His creation, bask in His presence. I can move forward.

There is grace for my doubt—every time. And that grace

leads me to recall His promises never to leave me or forsake me, which in turn pivots me toward confidence in His blessings of strength for today as well as continual grace and forgiveness for my annoying inability to learn from my repeat offenses of self-reliance. I pick myself up, brush off my doubt and worry and fear, and trust anew.

As I sought examples (there are many!) regarding my own shortcomings on this subject, I recalled a much more convicting illustration. Let's gain some insight from a long-ago adventure that went sideways. One that began in wonder but quickly and often resulted in aimless wandering. One that includes consequences, yes, but ultimately grace and joy. It is both a "cautionary tale" and an encouragement to trust God's promises.

World's Longest Road Trip

Approximately 3500 years ago, the Israelites set off on what could well have been an 11-day road trip. They made their escape from the bondage of slavery in Egypt, heading toward their ultimate destination, the promised land of Canaan. These were God's chosen people, and He provided all that was needed for a swift and successful journey, most notably His very real and powerful presence.

Each step of the way, the Israelites encountered seemingly insurmountable trials, but God blessed them with exactly what they needed when they needed it. Being chased by bad guys? No problem. God divided the sea and closed it up again just in the nick of time, all His chosen people safely on the other side. Hungry? God provided manna every day, the perfect food to satisfy their needs. Feeling alone and exposed? No problem! He provided His presence in the form of a cloud that went with them wherever they went. Wonder and provision at every turn and in every circumstance. They could trust Him. And they did, for short moments—until the next temptation or scary incident. Despite God's unfailing promises and unwavering support and protection of His people, the Israelites failed to get out of their own way, often unwilling to move forward in faith without fear.

To be fair, the heads and hearts of the Israelites were ready and willing at times, prepared and equipped to follow Moses, to heed God's calling for the lives of their entire people. How did it all go wrong? They sported a collective short memory, paired with lack of belief, and ultimately fear. Fear led to disobedience, and disobedience led to the only possible next step in the presence of God—consequence. It came in the form of delays, and SO. MUCH. WANDERING. Weeks stretched to years.

And then, no doubt weary but excited, they finally arrived just this side of the Jordan River, across from the promised destination of Canaan. I can't help but think God may have breathed a sigh of a relief of His own at that point, as He told them, *"See, I have given you this land. Go in and take possession of the land the Lord swore he would give to your fathers—to Abraham, Isaac and Jacob—and to their descendants after them."*[1] Finally!

But fear paralyzed them. Instead of crossing the river to take possession of what God had clearly promised them, they shrank back, consumed by doubt. They followed their own path, petitioning Moses to send ahead a contingent of a dozen spies to survey the land and confirm all was well. It became the 40-day investigative road trip within the road trip.

Fear Leads to Wandering

Upon their return, ten of the twelve men reported that while the land was indeed flowing with the promised milk and honey, it was also teeming with and controlled by giant and powerful men. These ten Israelite leaders obsessed about the sheer size of the problem, creating more fear and inciting the larger community to unbelief and lamenting. "Would it not be better for us to go back to Egypt?"[2]

With the benefit of a few millennia of hindsight, it seems so obvious. How could they leave no room for the power and wonder and promises of God, instead focusing on the choice to return to a life of slavery and a solution limited to their own strength? In his Bible commentary, J. Vernon McGee observes, "They left God out of the picture. If only they had put Him in, what a different story it would have been."

They questioned the entire exodus, dismissing all that God had provided and promised thus far. This chosen community, blessed by God and literally walking *with* Him, forgot they could trust Him enough to move forward.

The result? God punished those doubters, those fearful untrusting masses. He destined the older generation to wander in the wilderness, never to cross into the promised land. The consequence extended to the younger ones as well, now destined to wait almost four decades before God granted them entry to the Promised Land.

I look at these short-sighted, hand-wringing worriers, and I see me. It's so easy for me to leave God out of the picture, though I know in both my heart and my head that purposefully walking with Him leads to an experience filled with purpose. I falter despite my desire to seek wonder in the glory of His creation.

It often starts as doubt. First, there are the uncertainties that grab me before I ever leave the driveway. Did I budget well enough? What if my car breaks down in the middle of Kansas? What if I get sick? What if the weather is horrible for the entire trip? And then down the hole to, Why would I choose to travel by myself? Am I crazy? What am I doing??? It's a slippery slope from uncertainty to fear. I spiral into those places where I mildly panic, caught up only in my own inability to right the ship.

Inevitably, I will also find opportunity to panic or feel fear in the midst of my travels. And yet, I know God has called me to seek and find Him in the glory of His creation, and to encourage others, pointing them to Him as well. If I let these doubts and fears consume my day, I'm no better than the Israelites, robbed of both freedom and wonder, focusing only on what looks difficult or unpleasant. I miss the joy. I miss the blessing. My wonder reverts to wandering, and I stumble around, lacking purpose as well as peace.

I don't want to be a wilderness wanderer, doomed to anxiety. I want to be a Spirit-filled wonderer. I don't want to get caught up in worry and miss the joy. I don't want to allow anxiety to rule the day and miss the peace. I don't want to overthink each decision and miss the freedom.

But it happens. It's real. And it leads me down the wrong roads. You'll find yourself in the midst of self-made turmoil at some point. If not today, then when you're packing your car, or 500 miles from home. Remember that God didn't give us this spirit of fear, but He does provide a spirit of love and power and a strong mind.[3] That's the good stuff. That's the God stuff.

While the stakes on our personal adventures may not feel

comparable to the Exodus, the message is consistent. If God has led you to this place, He will bless both your tentative and strident steps forward.

Keep God's presence close to you, seek Him out as you explore, not seeking wonder in your own strength, but recognizing it is His creation that points you toward it. Go in hope and confidence.

Trust Leads to Wonder

In the story of the Israelites, ten lacked faith and incited doubt and fear into the masses. But what of the remaining two—Joshua and Caleb? Their response and the conclusions they drew stand in stark contrast to their doubting kinsmen:

"The land we passed through and explored is exceedingly good. If the Lord *is pleased with us, He will lead us into that land, a land flowing with milk and honey, and will give it to us. Only do not rebel against the* Lord. *And do not be afraid of the people of the land, because we will devour them. Their protection is gone, but the* Lord *is with us. Do not be afraid of them."*[4]

Do not fear. The Lord is with us. These two—only these two—chose to trust God. Consider the polarity of the responses: Twelve men took a journey, viewed the same fruitful land, and gaped at the same intimidatingly large giant-men. Ten returned full of fear, two undergirded with hope and conviction. As ten had neglected to take God along with them, their wanderings doomed them to death in the wilderness. Two kept their eyes open to the wonder God had already promised them, confident in His faithfulness. It's all perspective. Two chose to "take God with them" and look out with intention at what He might do. Ten fretted, convicted by fear and focusing on what they could not accomplish on their own.

Consider author Priscilla Shirer's reflection on the uniqueness, the "set apartness" of Joshua and Caleb's choice to move forward in hope, and its result.

"Abundant living mandates different living— different even from other believers who may be complacent with their freedom—lulled to sleep in their wilderness wandering. To experience everything God intends, a difference is required. One in which your thought processes, self- disciplines, and most pressing choices carve out a narrow road that is not often tread. One on which you will nearly always walk alone. Alien. Stranger. Sore Thumb."[5]

The narrow path—the daring to be different path. Caleb and Joshua wholeheartedly embraced the concept of the "road less traveled." Faced with giants and unable to grasp the details of how God would make good on His promise, they chose trust. God says that Caleb (and Joshua) had *"a different spirit and followed [Me] wholeheartedly."*[6] The narrow path resulted in blessing and abundance. Bravery was required, but not the man-made variety. It came from trusting the promise given by a God who had already proven Himself faithful over and over in their wanderings.

Unlike their fellow spies, Joshua and Caleb were rewarded with entry to the promised land of Canaan and a life of blessing and abundance. Their brave choice to trust God's

Word and lean not on their own understanding led them to the land that flowed with milk and honey. They continued lives already rich with the wonder of God's glory and His creation. They moved forward in the hope that comes from confidence because they remained in the will of God.

I want to be a Joshua or a Caleb. To go forward trusting God, seeking wonder, daring to be different. To be a wonderer with eyes wide open, following Him fully, without fear. To adventure with the confidence that He is with me, ever-present and faithful. The blessing is right there for the taking.

Trust Him for All of It

Forty years after God's people were condemned to wander in the wilderness, the debt was finally paid. That same Joshua stood poised to lead the nation of Israel across the Jordan and welcome them to the Promised Land. He must have been scared, despite his unfailing trust in God's faithfulness. After all these years, I'm sure he didn't want to mess up, potentially disappointing God as well as His people. In one short conversation, God tells him three times, "Be strong and courageous!" and then, "Do not be afraid; do not be discouraged, for the LORD your God will be with you wherever you go." I love that God consistently encouraged Him and provided Him with peace, reminding him he is not alone.

I believe we can adopt and heed that exact encouragement and promise for our own lives and by extension, for our adventures. Perhaps you feel as though you have been wandering in the desert on some level, uncertain how to move forward. It's okay to be scared, but don't become paralyzed by that fear, enmired in insecurity and doubt. It's so easy to get stuck in our heads, overthinking, overplanning, worrying, filled with anxiety. We allow our fear of the unknown to intensify to such a level that it outweighs our inherent spirit to be curious, to ask questions, to seek out new places and people—to adventure! Go forward in faith, in freedom, and in wonder!

A Final Inventory

As our time together draws to a close, let's take a step back. Not *backwards*, but back in the way artists step away to ensure they see their whole canvas, script, or story. It's a moment to gather thoughts and take inventory, to gently remind ourselves of all that we have learned. It's easy to become stuck on a particular concept or thought and lose the perspective of the big picture. Stepping back helps us regain our perspective, a gift when we become enmired in the details!

Even a cursory inspection affirms that the canvas is close to completion! In a nutshell, we have . . .

1. tackled and embraced the heart and the head elements of solo road-tripping.
2. deepened our understanding of the need for flexible planning, leaving plenty of opportunity for wonder.
3. fleshed out each of the practical pillars of adventuring while embracing the freedom to adjust according to our needs.
4. gained an appreciation for the necessities of packing and safe travel practices.
5. called out our inevitable fears and doubts and met them head on with trust and faith.

Well done you! We've cast a wide net, laying groundwork to recognize our desire to wonder-seek, to intentionally choose to step out and explore on our own terms. We took a deep dive into budget, navigation, packing, safety, etc.—all vital pieces of the puzzle. Let's step back now and see afresh. Let's appreciate how those necessary and important practicalities enhance our overall vision, providing confidence and calm as we forge toward freedom and wonder. Laying a foundation in which we've addressed the pragmatic gives us freedom to be glory-seekers, our eyes open to the beauty our God has created, beauty that points us back to Him—to chase down wonder that reminds us of His constant presence. Wonder is always the goal.

I think God instilled within each of us a sort of inner governor—a built-in hesitation before we release the brake and hit the gas. It's there to protect us from harm, but there's danger in that hesitation as well. Danger that when we idle safely, we may idle forever. John A. Shedd writes, "A ship in harbor is safe, but that is not what ships are built for." God did not create us to sit safely in the harbor, but to go. I love this encouragement from travel writer and editor Tim Cahill, as he speaks to our innate trepidation at striking out on our own.

" . . . the words 'Let's go!' are intrinsically courageous. It's the decision to go that is, in itself, entirely intrepid. We know from the first step that travel is often a matter of confronting our fear of the unfamiliar and the unsettling . . ."

But faith. But God. Part of embarking on a solo road trip requires bravely stepping out in faith and leaving fear in the dust. The blessings will be found in the stepping out, in being "strong and courageous." "The Lord your God will be with you wherever you go." So go ahead, take a step back, admire the canvas. You've created something beautiful! Now go in peace, in hope, looking up and out. There's wonder ahead.

Dog on Board!

He wasn't the most courageous of dogs. Nor, it must be said, was Henri very bright, but he was loyal beyond measure and knew what mattered . . . din-din, walks, but most of all his family. His heart filled his chest and ran to the end of his tail and the very tips of his considerable ears. It filled his head, squeezing out his brain . . . *Everything he knew, he knew by heart.*

—Louise Penny, *Bury Your Dead*

DOGS KNOW THEIR HUMANS WITH THEIR HEARTS. They long to please, comfort, provide solace, and simply love. They connect deeply with us, usually demanding little in return. While DNA and ancestry determine behaviors and traits that span the canine spectrum, every variety wears their hearts in their eyes. And in turn, we love them in part because of the way they love us.

It's the heart of Lexi the Golden that compels me to take her along for most of my adventures. She knows me by heart and has proven to be the most wonderful companion these past five years. While Lexi doesn't tag along on all my road trips, it's safe to say that she goes more often than she remains at home. In her young life she's logged almost 25,000 road-trip miles and marked territory in 30 states and Canada. My blond girl lives to swim, and she's chased sticks and stones in the Atlantic, the Pacific, and innumerable bodies of water between—sparkling lakes, freezing streams, rushing rivers. She is an equal opportunity swimmer.

In my estimation, Lexington Hope is a professional road-tripper. She loves every minute of it, I think. It can be difficult to read her mind at some junctures, but she goes along with almost everything, which seems a good sign. Our initial journey together transpired in part because I didn't want to leave my 9-month-old puppy for three weeks while I traveled west. Leaving her at home was also complicated, and we were already quite attached to one another. If you have a Golden this will resonate: I live with the presence of a furry shadow in my wake, watching, waiting, totally supportive, and a little bit needy. Parting for so long didn't feel right. Being away for three weeks felt like betrayal, so I decided to pack her up and take her for an extended "test drive."

In the months leading up to our travels, Lexi didn't really enjoy the car, occasionally getting sick and whimpering. I continued to take her on short rides, eventually building her endurance and willingness to ride for longer periods of time. By the time we headed west that summer, she was the quintessential travel buddy, though not exactly what I had envisioned—she wasn't the pup half hanging out the window, breeze blowing her ears back, toothy grin on her face. Turns out that's not Lexi's style, a little to my disappointment. She displays her pleasure with much less zeal. Occasionally I forget she's even with me. She is sentry-quiet, staring ahead or stretched sleepily across the back seat, dreaming of sticks and swimming holes as the miles tick by.

Lexi saves her sunny disposition for on-the-ground exploring. Once out of the car, traveling with Lexi is like playing second fiddle to a minor movie star. I become blissfully invisible as everyone fusses over her, offers treats, and asks to pose for photos. She embraces every moment. If we are in a small town, by Day Three half the inhabitants know her by name. It's a little weird. There's just something about this girl. She's confident, extraordinarily friendly (there are times she doesn't grasp the social cues when not *everyone* wants to love on her), and enjoys life on the road every single day.

Retaining the Wonder

Not all dogs take to the road as easily and happily as Lexi. I feel quite certain that my previous golden, Crosby, would not have been quite so trouble-free on a cross-country road trip. With Crosby, a quick run into Starbucks or a bathroom stop required locking down every morsel of food. He'd eat my entire Chick-fil-A meal (including the bag) in the time it takes to order a latté. The truth about Crosby, God rest his furry soul, was that he wasn't trouble-free in any situation! Traveling any lengthy distance with him would result in more frustration than joy, no matter how much I loved him. Not every dog can make the adjustment to travel buddy!

Adventuring together will alter your journey in many ways. As you consider teaming up, be intentional and realistic in thinking about how traveling with a dog in tow will alter and enhance your time on the road. The experience shouldn't sacrifice your pursuit of wonder, and it should absolutely be pleasant for both of you. Use this chapter to determine if the realities and responsibilities of traveling with a dog are more likely to enhance your eyes-wide-open journey of freedom and wonder or to distract you from it. Be honest with yourself!

As a stickler for language, I feel the need to unpack the idea of embarking on a "solo road trip with a dog." I don't believe this to be an oxymoron, as I am the only human on this adventure! I am alone to think, pray, and breathe in all that God has created for me to explore and absorb. From the practicalities of all the decision-making to the humbling moments of splendor, many of the joys of solo travel remain, despite the inclusion of another beating heart. Perfectly designed by the Creator God, Lexi adds joy without uttering thoughts or opinions—the quintessential silent partner.

I absolutely experience wonder with my four-legged friend. Her presence does not distract me from my pursuit of reveling in the glory of God's presence and creation. She also brings her own brand of wonder to the journey, enhancing our experience together.

Making a Wise Choice

We must move wonder and joy to the side for just a few moments as we consider the practical side of taking your dog on the road. For both your sake and that of the pup you love so much, please thoughtfully consider the benefits as well as the responsibilities of including your dog in your travels.

There are valid reasons why most people choose not to travel with their pets. It's more complicated, it can be more expensive, and pets who are poor travelers may be sick, miserable, and generally unhappy away from home. If it's not the right fit, having your dog with you can certainly be a detriment to your pursuit of freedom and wonder, tying you down and hindering you instead, while creating an unhappy experience for your faithful companion as well. We love them so much, and it's worth exploring whether both of you will be blessed by being together on the road.

Consider each of the following factors as you weigh your decision whether to include your dog on your road trip.

Temperament

- **Riding in the Car:** Does your dog enjoy being in the car for long periods of time? I purposely used the word "enjoy" and not "tolerate." It needs to be fun for them!

- **Barking:** Is your dog a barker? If so, consider the types of situations and places where this may be a problem for you, for your dog, or for others.

- **Size:** Does your vehicle provide enough room for your dog on longer trips? Also note that larger dogs may incur higher pet fees at hotels and are welcome in fewer places than small dogs.

- **Behavior:** Does your dog always come when called? Behave well around strangers? Is your dog aggressive in any way that may upset or harm strangers?

- **Walking/Hiking:** Is he great on a leash? Does he or she scare easily?

- **Sleeping:** Does your dog sleep easily in new and unfamiliar places?

- **Stimulation:** How does your dog handle meeting new people, encountering new dogs, and being in new places every day?

- **Anxiety:** does your dog get easily upset and anxious?

- **Storms:** is your dog afraid of storms and fireworks? How does she react?

- **Attachment:** can your dog handle being alone in the car for short periods, or alone at your place of lodging?

Physical Needs or Limitations

- **Exercise:** Most dogs are sedentary for many hours a day, which makes it easy to pop them in the car. But how much does your dog need to rip and tear, run and play each day? Does your version of a road trip align with the exercise needs of your dog?

- **Age and Mobility:** Can your dog hold his bladder well, or is he prone to occasional accidents? Can he get in and out of your vehicle easily? Does he get overheated or need an excess of water?

- **Special needs:** Does your dog need access to specific medicine, supplements, or any kind of training aids that may be difficult to carry with you?

- **Food:** Is your dog on a schedule that you need to keep

while traveling? Are food and medication easy to transport?

- **Vehicle:** Can you provide enough room for your dog to travel comfortably? Can you keep her cool/warm enough?

Adjusting Itinerary/Priorities

Traveling with your dog will impact many facets of your itinerary. It's vital to think through how your pet will affect the following:

- **Basic Itinerary:** Does your trip easily conform to the addition of a canine companion?

- **Hotel Cost:** Hotels almost always add a pet fee per night, though pet-friendly hotels are easy to find!

- **Activities:** Are the places you plan to visit welcoming to pets? Find out in advance!

- **Destination:** Whether it's a friend's house, Airbnb, hotel, etc., be certain that your sidekick is welcome.

- **Dining Out:** What kind of eating out do you plan to do, and can your dog do it with you?

- **Pet Priorities:** Are you willing to prioritize exercise for your dog each day, even if that means altering your plans?

Some Simple Pros and Cons

While not inclusive, consider this list as you contemplate including your dog in your journey. Not all items may apply to your situation, or you may discover that my upside would be a drawback for you. Your adventure is completely unique to you!

Potential Upsides	Possible Drawbacks
Quiet companionship	More planning required
Safety/protection (real or perceived)	More expensive hotels (pet fees)
Great photo ops/videos	Limits destinations (restaurants, shopping, some trails, museums, ball parks, etc.)
Easier to talk to people/make friends	Limits lodging/rental options
Hiking buddy	More space required for dog and dog gear
Camping buddy	Inability to leave dog in car when hot
Joy in being together	Dog may not be willing to travel long hours, particularly when traveling many days
Carefree camaraderie	Car sickness, etc. Yuck.
Increases comfort level for doing some things you may feel weird doing alone	Needy/unhappy dogs may whine, cry, and bark continually

Pet Friendliness on the Rise

Traveling with a four-legged "plus one" will limit some of your restaurant, activity, and lodging choices, although our culture has become so dog crazy that our canine friends are invited into more places than ever before. In the aftermath of Covid, I have noticed a significant upswing in dog-friendly establishments of all kinds, which is good news for road-tripping with your pooch!

Bring Fido
Many places do not welcome dogs of any kind unless you

have a bona fide service dog. Invest a bit of time to ensure your itinerary meshes with destinations that allow dogs. A wonderful resource to find pet-friendly establishments is the BringFido app and website. If you're traveling with your pet, you need this! Among other things, it allows you to type in a location to access all the nearby pet-friendly accommodations and eating establishments, usually with some helpful details. I have found it to be quite dependable over the years. You can use BringFido to mine for ideas or book your pet-friendly hotels directly on the site. They also offer information on local events, pet-friendly trails, dog parks and dog-friendly stores, as well as local vets and groomers. It's a free service and constantly being updated.

Lodging

Many more hotels are now pet-friendly, though there is almost always a pet fee. Some Airbnbs welcome well-behaved dogs and will typically provide a written pet policy. I've encountered a few that truly cater to pets! Last summer Lexi and I stayed in a cute little house in a small town in North Dakota. The owner supplied dog bowls, a dog bed, towels for wiping muddy paws, extra dog food, and an entire plate of homemade dog treats for Lexi! In my experience, more rural locations tend to be dog-friendly, though it's not always the case. Airbnb, Vrbo and HipCamp all have a filter in their search engines specifically for pets, which saves me from pawing needlessly through results to determine whether Lexi is welcome or not.

Most campgrounds do not charge extra for dogs, and almost all have at least some pet friendly sites. Camping with a dog is fun and can provide an added feeling of safety and security when you're alone. Lexi loves sitting around the fire and snuggling in the tent, and she always makes plenty of new friends!

Restaurants

In the past few years, the number of pet-friendly restaurants seems to be on the rise. While dining with your dog usually limits you to the patio or deck, it's not unusual to see well-behaved dogs curled up under the table. Many establishments will provide bowls of water and dog treats as well.

Occasionally, I encounter an uber dog-friendly place to eat. In these restaurants, the dog's dining experience has been given equal consideration to that of its owner. A wonderful example is The Gettysburger in downtown Gettysburg, Pennsylvania. After a long walk through the battlefield with your four-legged friend, you can enjoy the cozy tables along the alley where your dog gets his own menu! Lexi has rarely been fussed over to the extent she is when we visit this little spot. Most recently, a neighboring table asked if they could buy her dessert. The bowl of ice cream was gobbled in less than ten seconds. I do wonder if dogs get brain freeze.

Dining out with your dog also makes for easy conversation-starters, and while many patrons love to fuss over an unexpected pup out for dinner, you will also encounter those who do not love the experience of a dog nosing up to their table. Make sure you're confident in your dog's ability to sit quietly and refrain from disturbing other customers. I find eating out with Lexi is almost always a great experience. I struggle a bit with the prospect of dining alone so having her by my side increases my comfort level considerably!

Shopping

I've found that dog-friendly shopping is pretty hit-and-miss, though in my personal experience, the West and Pacific Northwest tend to be the most dog-friendly areas of the country. I generally assume that pets are not welcome, but if the local vibe seems quite dog friendly, I will ask. Occasionally, if I encounter a business I truly wish to visit, I poke my head in the door and inquire if dogs are welcome. I'm always surprised when the answer is "yes" and have determined it's worth asking! Lexi has enjoyed air-conditioned bliss in quite a few shops across America, most recently in the famous Vermont Country Store in Weston, Vermont, where she was quite enamored with the cheese counter!

Hiking

While it may seem a given that dogs would be welcome on hiking trails, it's not always the case. National parks, in particular, are very selective about whether patrons are permitted to hike with dogs. In most cases, denial of a dog on the trails is for the protection of the dog as well as the local wildlife and fauna. Encountering a grizzly bear or a protective mama moose is less than ideal when hiking with a dog in tow, no matter how cool the park or gorgeous the view.

There are several national parks and many state and local parks that do allow dogs. A few of the most notable locations include Sedona in Arizona, Acadia National Park in Maine, and Shenandoah National Park in Virginia. Within each park, you may find both trails that permit dogs and those that don't, so be sure to check in advance. In some areas, a dog can be off-leash, but before letting her run, be sure her recall is extremely dependable.

My favorite resource for hiking is the AllTrails app or website. A paid version of the app is available for avid hikers, though the free version is great! You can search for hikes in any given area, read user reviews, see photos, determine the length and elevation of hikes, and read rules for dogs on the trail.

Prepping to Take Your Dog on the Road

Regardless of all the wonder and potential (literal) mountain-top experiences, the most important moment of traveling with your beloved pet is returning home safely together. Investing some time and forethought in how to successfully integrate your pal into your adventure will go a long way toward a safe homecoming. Even if you tend to fly by the seat of your pants, including your pooch requires a bit of planning!

Before You Go

- **Visit the Vet:** Make sure your pup has a clean bill of health before you go, and update any needed vaccinations, especially rabies! Refill any supplements or medications you may need and ensure your dog is up to date on flea and tick prevention. Let the vet know your plans as he/she may have some additional tips for you.

- **Take a Few Test Drives:** If your pup doesn't travel with you regularly, start including him on your daily rounds, short and long drives, etc. The car shouldn't be a novelty when you set off on your road trip, nor should it connote only negative experiences, like going somewhere stressful or unenjoyable. Invest time to make sure your dog is comfortable, relaxed, and happy to be in the car.

- **Prep Your Vehicle:** Determine a strategy for how your dog will travel in your vehicle. Consistency will be a friend to you both, so create a plan and stick to it. Dogs, like children, need routine, especially when the rest of their surroundings will be unfamiliar and changing. They also need a space to call their own.

Begin by determining what area the dog will occupy. You may choose to crate your dog for maximum ease and safety or provide them with a back seat where they have freedom to move a bit. Some owners purchase tethers or harnesses that are designed specifically for securing a dog to the seat. These provide some freedom of movement while increasing the level of safety in case of an accident.

You can also purchase a divider that will always keep your dog behind you. We love having them near us, but we must be free to drive without distraction. If your dog roams, regardless of size and intention, he will distract you and impede your ability to drive safely.

In almost every state, it is unlawful for a dog to sit on an owner's lap while the owner is driving, and in some jurisdictions, dogs must be tethered for safety. Check the resources for links regarding additional travel precautions and safety.

If your dog is traveling on a seat, consider purchasing a seat cover! I personally favor the "nest" style covers, which not only protect the entire back seat from dirt, dog hair, and all the other yummy things Lexi drags into the car, but create a comfortable cocoon of sorts for her. The design includes straps that snap around the headrests of the rear seat as well as the back of both front seats. She remains comfortable, and the material is easily wiped off and washable!

- **Packing for Your Pooch:** I've included Lexi's complete

packing list in the resources, though some specific needs will vary from one spoiled dog to the next! Here are just a few main items to get started.

Most dogs will sleep a great deal in the car, so including toys, bones, and other fun items may not be necessary. If your dog has a favorite toy or blanket, do take it. Regardless of where we may lay our heads at night, something from home helps us all sleep better!

Be sure you have room for dog food, water, and bowls. These can take up a good bit of space. Pack them so they are easily accessible for you throughout your travels, yet out of reach for your inquisitive pooch.

Safety Tips

I treasure Lexi's mostly silent companionship when we are on the road together. I do think about those moments, however, when it would be incredibly helpful for her to speak up! Imagined scenarios where she could become lost or we could be separated have motivated me to build in some emergency protocols. Here are a few measures to help in scary situations. I've included specific recommendations and lists in the resources.

- **Dog Tag ID:** Be sure your dog's collar includes a tag that states your dog's name and your cell phone number.

- **"In Case of Emergency" Access:** In your emergency envelope in your car, include specific pet information and instructions in case there is an accident and you are not able to speak for yourself.

- **Locator:** Attach a tracking device to your pet's collar. These typically work with smartphones or have their own remotes.

- **First Aid Kit:** I carry doggy first aid items and keep them in my hiking pack since a walk or hike is when she's most likely to become injured or need assistance. The contents are not extensive but having liquid Benadryl in case of a bee sting, for example, can be the difference between a quick recovery and a very complicated and scary situation.

Day in the Dog Life

Steinbeck set off from Sag Harbor on the morning of September 23, 1960, with Charley, his tall and gregarious French poodle, for company. "I remember when he asked to take Charley Dog," his wife later recalled. "He said rather meekly, 'This is a big favor I'm going to ask, Elaine. Can I take Charley?' 'What a good idea,' I said, 'if you get into any kind of trouble, Charley can go get help.' John looked at me sternly and said, 'Elaine, Charley isn't Lassie.'"

—Jay Parini, from the
Introduction of Travels with Charley

So what's it really like to travel extensively with a dog? The answer will differ for every dog/human partnership from now until the end of time. I can share a bit of my own experience with my girl, which may inspire you to give it a try or convince you to travel solo—no dogs allowed!

Lexi certainly adds a different dynamic to my adventures. Logistically, there have been moments when it would have been easier to be alone, but she brings her own brand of wonder to the road that supersedes most inconveniences. However, if I'm taking a trip that wouldn't be fun for her and would lead to a navigational nightmare for me, she stays home. I know there will be a day when her body won't allow her to go, but hopefully that day is far in the future. For now, we will enjoy every moment possible! Here are a few of my favorite and least favorite realities of traveling with Lexi the Golden.

The Good Stuff

I know she is her happiest when she is with me. We've been together since she was nine weeks old, and most of that time it's been only the two of us. Our personalities are similar, which makes all our time together fairly simple, regardless of where we may be.

- Lexi doesn't really bark much at all (except at statues of Civil War generals rising unexpectedly in the middle of a battlefield) and thankfully she's not destructive. I can leave her unattended in a hotel room or rental without worrying she's tearing the place up or annoying any neighbors.

- She's amazing in the car and remains patient and content whether we travel short distances or long. On days-long drives back from the West, I tend to drive 12–14-hour days as I'm ready to just be home. Somehow, she knows, and I barely hear a peep from the back seat during those long hauls.

- I meet more people because of Lexi, which is almost always a positive! I tend to be more introverted, and she is most definitely not. She can spot a sucker with a treat a mile away and is never shy about approaching anyone she deems friendly.

- I believe she would protect me if the need ever arose. She's not aggressive in any way, though I did discover quite by accident that she absolutely did not appreciate a stranger running up to our vehicle as I drove away from a gas station, even if was only to kindly inform me that my tailgate was open. She growled and barked and showed her teeth. I thought she'd lost her mind. Golden retrievers are more likely to lick a stranger to death than bare their teeth and I expected her lover to override her fighter nearly always, but she proved me wrong that day. Good girl!

The Hard Stuff

- If I'm in a town where I'd love to do a deep dive into the shops or museums, or sit down in a nice cool restaurant, I have to just say no and move on.

- Extreme heat is hard on her, and it can be challenging to stay out of the elements on those incredibly hot days. Where I might be content to walk through a town when it's 90 degrees, she is not, which can alter plans.

- There's always a risk of injury to one of us when we're hiking. I can't carry her, and she can't really help me either! We haven't had to cross that bridge, but I do think about it, and I tend to choose trails where it's likely we will encounter other hikers.

- Dogs do get sick and injured. Lexi went lame last year when we were in Wyoming. I have no idea what happened or what was actually wrong. When we arrived at our cabin for the night, she wouldn't put any weight on one leg, and refused to walk anywhere. I couldn't find a local vet who would see her. Sadly, it altered our Teton Forest hiking plan, but I was grateful she recovered in a few days and we moved on.

- I use extreme caution when leaving her in the car

when temperatures are warmer. It's unavoidable to have to stop for a bathroom or to run into a store. If an establishment does not allow Lexi to join me and I feel it is safe to leave her briefly, I do take precautions by parking in the shade or where the sun isn't beating into the car. I put the windows down a bit (I often open the sunroof entirely if it doesn't make things worse), make sure she has access to water, and turn on a battery-operated fan that attaches to the headrest in front of her.

Prior to leaving home, it is important to talk to your vet to map a plan that will ensure the safety and comfort of your own dog as you travel.

Dog Wonder

The hope and thrill of encountering these God-moments remains at the heart of the journey. I've discovered that traveling with Lexi adds to the opportunities for wonder. I'm always amazed that she can smell and sense water long before we can see it. Her fascination with small children causes me to slow down and see things through their eyes, trading giggles for sloppy kisses. Her ability to charm a barista or a small collection of college students makes me take notice of each of their faces, ringed in smiles. Surely, I would have wandered past them had it not been for her joy in greeting each, and receiving belly rubs and treats in return. Swimming and swimming and swimming—in streams so icy my feet can only handle a few seconds, and in the calm expanse of Montana lakes filled with jewel-colored stones I may have missed had she not waited for me to throw one, then another, then dozens as she chased the plops and splashes, quickly dogpaddling back in anticipation of the next.

While she's oblivious to many of the wonders I encounter in this world, she revels and delights in the fascination of her own doggie brand. For me it's double the beauty as I'm blessed by two dimensions of joy.

> Additional tips, resources, and information on road-tripping with your dog can be found at: www.wonderbingtravel.com/book-resources

Acknowledgments

While this book was conceived in the dark solitude of a West Virginia highway, bringing it into the light has required the goodwill and generosity of a small but willing army.

For every heart that beats behind the names printed here, there is a story of grace folding them seamlessly into this story. Some stepped in and out quickly, inadvertently playing their part, but most have remained for the long haul. No words will be adequate to properly thank any of them, but I will endeavor to try.

Kathy Jo, this never ever happens without you. How marvelous is our God who "randomly" determined we would become "sisters" in 1984. Our own path together winds through mountaintops and deep valleys, with you usually shining the light ahead. I absolutely would not and could not have seen this project to its end if you hadn't willingly answered all the phone calls and responded to every text.

To my beloved college roommate turned editor. Darce, God always knew how this would go, even in the great gap of time. While I will forever grieve the loss of those years, His grace and mercy is abundantly clear in our present. Thank you for every late night and early morning, every text, email, voicemail, Zoom, and Marco Polo ☺. Your encouragement and expertise are treasures in all of this!

To my generous "beta readers". I wish I had coined a lovelier term to describe the great gift you each gave of your time, care, and honesty with every page. Marlene, Elaine, Karen and Kim—I am forever grateful.

Great thanks to the experts! Michelle, you completely bought into my vision and made it so much more than I imagined. And Renee, endless thanks as you navigated me through the process to ensure the book will be found by others who may need it. I would have never hit the "publish" button without you both! And finally, to my mom and sister who painstakingly proofread every word. An extraordinary blessing.

Writing this book meant doing a deep and not always pleasant dive into everything that brought me to this place where I can now offer help and encouragement to others. It also gave me free license to reflect on the pivotal moments and central characters who played a part in my journey to wonder . . .

To the Binger clan—my story is also yours in so many ways. I hope I recounted those parts well. If not, I'm sure you'll tell me. ☺

My two very favorites, Sarah and Will (and Josh!)—thank you for never telling me that I'm crazy and for supporting my odd little dream. This life isn't what any of us imagined, and I'm grateful for every hard-fought moment. I'm so incredibly proud of you guys.

Jill, thank you for moving to Italy all those years ago. I don't think I write this book without your move and your contagious sense of adventure. Those years hold some of my most precious memories of our girls and of us. I treasure our friendship and all the places it has taken us!

To the rest of the posse who has unfailingly encouraged me and cheered me on, especially in these past six years: LJ, Denise, Templin, Erin, Brianne, Marchal & Brad, and my other Jill (& Jerry!). I love you all!

There is wonder in creation, but also in people. You are each a wonder to me!

About the Author

Beth Binger is on a mission to equip and inspire women to confidently step into a new season of life by planning and embarking on a solo road trip. Through her YouTube channel, blog, and now her new book, Beth shares and teaches women the practicalities of solo travel, but more importantly, how to leave confusion and uncertainty in the rear view as they seek freedom and wonder.

Beth and her beloved retriever, Lexi the Golden, have road tripped over 50,000 miles and through 46 states to date. Forever known as Bing to friends, "Mom" remains her favorite name, thanks to her two treasured adult children and an amazing son-in-law. When she's not on the road, home is a Civil War era farmhouse just up the road from Gettysburg.

End Notes

Foreword

1. John Steinbeck, *Travels with Charley* (New York: Penguin Books, 2017), 95.

Chapter 1: Priming for Wonder

1. Jeremy Camp, vocalist, "Keep Me in the Moment," by Jeremy Camp, Matthew West, and Jordan Sapp, CMG Song # 206916, Only in You Publishing (SESAC), Capital CMG Paragon (BMI), Capital CMG Amplifier (SESAC), © 2019. All rights reserved. Used by permission.

Chapter 2: Wonder

1. The first biblical account of creation can be found in Genesis 1 and 2, Genesis 1 giving an overview and Genesis 2 highlighting the sixth day work.

2. Sarah Young, *Jesus Calling: Enjoying Peace in His Presence* (Nashville: Thomas Nelson, 2008), November 16 entry, 335.

3. "Taste and see that the Lord is good; blessed is the one who takes refuge in Him." Psalm 34:8 (New International Version).

4. "Now unto Him that is able to keep you from falling, and to present you faultless before the presence of His glory with exceeding joy." Jude 24 (King James Version).

Chapter 3: A Pause to Wonder *Why*

1. Ann Voskamp, *One Thousand Gifts* (Zondervan, 2010), 69.

Chapter Four: An Affair of the Heart

1. *Yellowstone*, "Cigarettes, Whiskey, a Meadow and You," season 5, episode 6, aired December 11, 2022, Paramount Network, https://www.paramountnetwork.com/shows/yellowstone.

2. Emily P. Freeman, *A Million Little Ways*, (Revell, 2013), 108.

3. Freeman, *A Million Little Ways*, 110-11.

Chapter Five: The Treasure Map

1. William Least Heat-Moon, *Blue Highways: A Journey into America*, (Little, Brown and Company, 2013), 6.

Chapter Six: Going Solo

1. Bradley Williams, "45+ Female Travel Statistics (2024!)," *Dream Big Travel Far* (blog), February 26, 2024, https://www.dreambigtravelfarblog.com/blog/female-travel-statistics.

2. Sarah Young, *Jesus Calling: Enjoying Peace in His Presence* (Nashville: Thomas Nelson, 2008), January 9 entry, 10.

3. Ann Voskamp, *The Greatest Gift: Unwrapping the Full Love Story of Christmas*, (Tyndale, 2013), 125.

Chapter Seven: Mini Wonderings

1. Emily P. Freeman, *A Million Little Ways*, (Revell, 2013), 102.

2. "Have I not commanded you? Be strong and courageous. Do not be frightened, and do not be dismayed, for the Lord your God is with you wherever you go." Joshua 1:9 (English Standard Version)

Chapter Eight: Personal Peace

1. "Do not be anxious about anything, but in everything by prayer and supplication with thanksgiving let your requests be made known to God. And the peace of God, which surpasses

all understanding, will guard your hearts and your minds in Christ Jesus." Philippians 4:6-7 (English Standard Version)

Chapter Nine: Big Picture Planning

1. "Trust in the Lord with all your heart, and do not lean on your own understanding. In all your ways acknowledge Him, and He will make straight your paths." Proverbs 3:5-6 (English Standard Version)

Chapter Twelve: Time and Distance

1. Sarah Young, *Jesus Calling: Enjoying Peace in His Presence* (Nashville: Thomas Nelson, 2008), February 17 entry, 50.

2. Sarah Young, *Jesus Calling: Enjoying Peace in His Presence* (Nashville: Thomas Nelson, 2008), March 16 entry, 79.

Chapter Fourteen: Lodging

1. John Steinbeck, *Travels with Charley* (New York: Penguin Books, 2017), page 93.

Chapter Eighteen: The Missing Pieces—Faith and Trust

1. "See, I have given you this land. Go in and take possession of the land the Lord swore he would give to your fathers—to Abraham, Isaac and Jacob—and to their descendants after them." Deuteronomy 1:8 (New International Version)

2. "Would it not be better for us to go back to Egypt?" Numbers 14:3b (English Standard Version)

3. "For God has not given us a spirit of fear, but of power and of love and of a sound mind." 2 Timothy 1:7 (New King James Version)

4. "The land we passed through and explored is exceedingly good. If the Lord is pleased with us, He will lead us into that land, a land flowing with milk and honey, and will give it to us. Only do not rebel against the Lord. And do not be afraid of the people of the land, because we will devour them. Their

protection is gone, but the Lord is with us. Do not be afraid of them." Numbers 1: 7b-9 (New International Version)

5. Priscilla Shirer, *Awaken: 90 Days with the God Who Speaks,* "The Difference," (Nashville: B&H Books, 2017), Day 40, 10.

6. "But because my servant Caleb has a different spirit and follows me wholeheartedly, I will bring him into the land he went to, and his descendants will inherit it." Numbers 14:24 (New International Version)

To find my own blog posts referenced in this book or to read more about my specific travels, visit: https://justbeingbing.com/

Blog posts from Nomadic Matt can be found at: https://www.nomadicmatt.com/.

Fellow wonderers,

I hope you have grown in confidence and excitement with each chapter of *There's Wonder Around the Bend*. But the equipping doesn't end here! Please check out the links below to join a growing community of women who are seeking wonder as they move forward in their lives. My website offers additional opportunities for support and camaraderie as you step into your own journey of freedom and wonder.

Additionally, my YouTube channel and social networks provide weekly tips, stories, and road tripping education.

And finally, *your* stories are so important to this endeavor! As you embark on your solo journey, I hope you will share your adventures with us all!

Join the Facebook Group The WonderBings https://www.facebook.com/groups/thewonderbings or share with me personally at bing@wonderbingtravel.com.

Blessings for the road ahead,

Beth / Bing

Website: wonderbingtravel.com

YouTube: https://www.youtube.com/@WonderBingTravel

Instagram: instagram.com/wonderbingtravel

Facebook: facebook.com/wonderbingtravel